access to

FRANCE *in* REVOLUTION

Second Edition

TA

ι

Dylan Rees and Duncan Townson

ıghton

DLINE GROUP

Acknowledgements

The front cover illustration shows *La Liberté* by Nanine Vallain (courtesy La Museé de la Revolution Française, Vizelle).

The publishers would like to thank the following individuals, institutions and companies for permission to reproduce copyright illustrations in this book: Archivo Iconografico/Corbis, page 91; Bibliothèque Nationale , pages 13, 19, 51, 95 and 120; *The Taking of the Bastille, 14 July 1789* (oil on canvas) by French School (18th Century) Château de Versailles, France/Bridgeman Art Library, page 28; *The Tragic End of the Life of King Louis XVI (1754–93)*, 21st January 1793 (engraving) by French School (18th Century), Musée de la Revolution Française, Vizille, France/Bridgeman Art Library, page 68; Hulton Archive, page 64.

The publishers would also like to thank the following for permission to reproduce material in this book: Blackwell Publishers for the extract from *The Revolution Against the Church: from Reason to Supreme Being* by M. Vovelle, Polity Press, 1991; Cambridge University Press for the extract from *Interpreting the French Revolution* by Furet, Cambridge University Press, 1981 and the graph from *The French Revolution: An Economic Interpretation* by F. Aftalion, Cambridge University Press, 1990; Hodder & Stoughton for the extracts from *The French Revolution: the Fall of the Ancien Regime to the Thermidorian Reaction 1785–1797* by John Hardman, Arnold, 1981, *Louis XVI* by John Hardman, Arnold, 2000 and *The French Revolution 1789–99* by E.G. Rayner and R.F. Stapley, Hodder & Stoughton, 1990; Orion Publishing Group for the extract from *The French Revolution* by George Rude, Weidenfeld & Nicolson, 1988; the extract from *The Oxford History of the French Revolution* by W. Doyle, Oxford University Press, 1989, by permission of Oxford University Press; the extract from *Religion and Revolution in France 1780–1804* by Nigel Aston, Macmillan, 2000, reproduced with permission of Palgrave; Pearson Education for the extracts from *The Origins of the French Revolutionary Wars* by T.C.W. Blanning, Longman, 1986, *The Reign of Terror in France: Jean-Baptiste Carrier and the Drownings of* Nantes by Josh Brooman, Longman, 1986, *Napoleon* by G. Ellis, Longman, 1997, and *Revolution and Terror in France* by D.G. Wright, Longman, 1981; Routledge for the extract from *The French Revolution: Rethinking the Debate* by G. Lewis, Routledge, 1993; the University of Wales Press for the extract from *Napoleon Comes to Power* by M. Crook, University of Wales Press, 1998; Yale University Press for the extract from *A Cultural History of the French Revolution* by Emmet Kennedy, © 1989 by Emmet Kennedy, Yale University Press, 1989.

Every effort has been made to trace and acknowledge ownership of copyright. The publishers will be glad to make suitable arrangements with any copyright holders whom it has not been possible to contact.

Orders: please contact Bookpoint Ltd, 78 Milton Park, Abingdon, Oxon OX14 4TD. Telephone (44) 01235 827720, Fax: (44) 01235 400454. Lines are open from 9.00–6.00, Monday to Saturday, with a 24 hour message answering service. Email address: orders@bookpoint.co.uk

British Library Cataloguing in Publication Data
A catalogue record for this title is available from the British Library

ISBN 0 340 803 274

First published 2001

Impression number	10 9 8 7 6 5 4 3 2 1
Year	2007 2006 2005 2004 2003 2002 2001

Copyright © 2001 Dylan Rees and Duncan Townson

Typeset by Fakenham Photosetting Limited, Fakenham, Norfolk
Printed in Great Britain for Hodder & Stoughton Educational, a division of Hodder Headline Plc, 338 Euston Road, London NW1 3BH by Bath Press Limited, England.

Contents

Preface

The original *Access to History* series was conceived as a collection of sets of books covering popular chronological periods in British history, together with the histories of other countries, such as France, Germany, Russia and the USA. This arrangement complemented the way in which history has traditionally been taught in sixth forms, colleges and universities. In recent years, however, other ways of dividing up the past have become increasingly popular. In particular, there has been a greater emphasis on studying relatively brief periods in considerable detail and on comparing similar historical phenomena in different countries. These developments have generated a demand for appropriate learning materials, and, in response, two new 'strands' have been added to the main series – *In Depth* and *Themes*. The new volumes build directly on the features that have made *Access to History* so popular.

To the general reader

Access books have been specifically designed to meet the needs of examination students, but they also have much to offer the general reader. The authors are committed to the belief that good history must not only be accurate, up-to-date and scholarly, but also clearly and attractively written. The main body of the text (excluding the Study Guide sections) should therefore form a readable and engaging survey of a topic. Moreover, each author has aimed not merely to provide as clear an explanation as possible of what happened in the past but also to stimulate readers and to challenge them into thinking for themselves about the past and its significance. Thus, although no prior knowledge is expected from the reader, he or she is treated as an intelligent and thinking person throughout. The author tends to share ideas and explore possibilities, instead of delivering so-called 'historical truths' from on high.

To the student reader

It is intended that *Access* books should be used by students studying history at a higher level. Its volumes are all designed to be working texts, which should be reasonably clear on a first reading but which will benefit from re-reading and close study.

To be an effective and successful student, you need to budget your time wisely. Hence you should think carefully about how important the material in a particular book is for you. If you simply need to acquire a general grasp of a topic, the following approach will probably be effective:

1. Read Chapter 1, which should give you an overview of the whole book, and think about its contents.
2. Skim through Chapter 2, paying particular attention to the *Points to Consider* box and to the *Key Issue* highlighted at the start of each section. Decide if you need to read the whole chapter.
3. If you do, read the chapter, stopping at the end of every sub-division of the text to make notes.
4. Repeat stage 2 (and stage 3 where appropriate) for the other chapters.

If, however, your course demands a detailed knowledge of the contents of the book, you will need to be correspondingly more thorough. There is no perfect way of studying, and it is particularly worthwhile experimenting with different styles of note-making to find the one that best suits you. Nevertheless the following plan of action is worth trying:

1. Read a whole chapter quickly, preferably at one sitting. Avoid the temptation – which may be very great – to make notes at this stage.
2. Study the diagram at the end of the chapter, ensuring that you understand the general 'shape' of what you have read.
3. Re-read the chapter more slowly, this time taking notes. You may well be amazed at how much more intelligible and straightforward the material seems on a second reading – and your notes will be correspondingly more useful to you when you have to write an essay or revise for an exam. In the long run, reading a chapter twice can, in fact, often save time. Be sure to make your notes in a clear, orderly fashion, and spread them out so that, if necessary, you can later add extra information.
4. The Study Guide sections will be particularly valuable for those taking AS Level, A Level and Higher. Read the advice on essay questions, and do tackle the specimen titles. (Remember that if learning is to be effective, it must be active. No one – alas – has yet devised any substitute for real effort. It is up to you to make up your own mind on the key issues in any topic.)
5. Attempt the *Source-based questions* section. The guidance on tackling these exercises is well worth reading and thinking about.

When you have finished the main chapters, go through the 'Further Reading' section. Remember that no single book can ever do more than introduce a topic, and it is to be hoped that, time permitting, you will want to read more widely. If *Access* books help you to discover just how diverse and fascinating the human past can be, the series will have succeeded in its aim – and you will experience that enthusiasm for the subject which, along with efficient learning, is the hallmark of the best students.

Keith Randell

1 The *Ancien Régime*

POINTS TO CONSIDER

This chapter will introduce you to the nature and structure of French society before 1789, and to some of its leading critics. You should try to assess the problems and tensions which existed between the various sections of society, and to decide why the King's government was unable to operate effectively and efficiently. It is also important that you try to understand the nature of the arguments of the critics. You will encounter many new words and phrases. Refer to the glossary to help you understand what they mean.

KEY DATES

1731 Voltaire a leading critic of the Church published *Lettres Philosophiques*
1748 Montesqieu published *'Spirit of the Laws'*
1752 First volume of *The Encyclopaedia* edited by Diderot
1762 Rousseau's *'Social Contract'* stated that 'men are born free but are everywhere in chains'
1766 Louis XV declared that sovereign power rested with the monarch alone

1 Introduction

In France during the *ancien régime*, the only way to remove an absolute ruler was by means of violence. The punishment for any successful or unsuccessful assassin was horrific. Torture was used to extract a confession and to determine whether the act was part of a conspiracy or not. A favoured method of torture was an iron boot, placed on the foot of the victim and then tightened gradually until, the bones were crushed. Henry IV's assassin, Ravaillac, suffered an unimaginably painful, two-stage public torture in 1610. Large crowds assembled at the place de Grève, in Paris to witness the spectacle. During the first stage the arm with which the assassin stabbed and killed the king, was plunged into burning sulphur. The flesh on his chest, arms and legs was torn by red-hot pincers. Then molten lead, boiling oil and a mixture of molten wax and sulphur were poured into the wounds. This stage lasted an hour or so. The second stage involved tying the assassin's arms and legs to four horses which then pulled in different directions. Following this stage the victim died, after which his body was torn into pieces by the mob.[1] A variation of this procedure was used on Damiens, the unsuccessful assassin who stabbed Louis XV in 1757.

The state which organized these punishments would itself be brought down by means of violent protest.[2] There have been few more dramatic events in modern European history than the French Revolution. The young romantic poet William Wordworth summed up what the revolution meant for someone of his generation, 'Bliss was it in that dawn to be alive, But to be young was very heaven'.[3]

The study of the French Revolution has produced a vast number of books and articles, in many different languages – an ever expanding pool of knowledge. All this can appear very daunting to any student studying the subject for the first time. So many important events were crammed into a period of 13 years (1787–99) and so many leading figures emerged only to be quickly replaced (and often eliminated), that bewilderment can quickly follow one's initial contact with the subject. The aims of this book are to identify the important themes and issues, and provide you with a clear explanation of what occurred during the revolution. Where possible, contemporary sources will be provided as part of the narrative, and the views of historians used to support the analysis. A range of tasks and exercises is given to enable you to test your understanding of the content, and to help measure your progress.

2 The King's Government

> **KEY ISSUE** What were the main problems which confronted the King's government during the *ancien régime?*

The '*ancien régime*' was an expression in common use by 1790 to describe the French system of government, laws and institutions which preceded the Revolution of 1789. An examination of this society is necessary if you are to understand how the Revolution came about. It is also important to know what the administrative structure of France was like under the *ancien régime*, so that you can assess the significance of the changes which the Constituent Assembly brought about between 1789 and 1791.

The kings of France were absolute in that their authority was not limited by any representative body, such as a parliament. They were responsible only to God. Louis XV expressed this view when, in 1766, he said: 'sovereign power resides in my person alone . . . the power of legislation belongs to me alone – it is not dependent on or shared with anyone else.' The King could imprison anyone without bringing him to trial by issuing a *lettre de cachet* (the *cachet* was a wax seal). Yet the French monarchy was not despotic (having total power). They were bound by the laws and customs of his kingdom and there were many independent bodies, like the Assembly of the Clergy, which had rights and privileges which the King could not interfere with, as they were guaranteed by the law. The King made laws after consulting his councils of advisers, though he was not bound to accept their views.

Considerable power was in the hands of a few ministers. The Controller-General was the most important of these, as he was in charge of the royal finances. There was no cabinet, where ministers could meet to make decisions in common. Each of them dealt with the King individually. Nor was there a prime minister, as the King would never tolerate a minister whose power might rival his own.

In the provinces the King's government was carried on by the *intendants* of police, of justice and of finance. They were appointed by and directly responsible to the King, who gave them wide powers in the 34 *généralités* (financial units) into which France was divided. They supervised the collection of taxes and the practice of religion. They also enforced law and order and were responsible for public works, communications, commerce and industry.

The main direct tax before the revolution was the *taille*. In theory it was payable by anyone who did not belong to one or other of the two privileged estates – the Church and the Nobility. However in reality, because of exemptions granted to towns it fell mainly on the peasantry. There were also the *capitation* (a poll tax on individuals) and the *vingtième* (a five per cent levy on all incomes). However, there was no uniformity in the imposition of these taxes. The church did not pay them at all, and nobles did not pay the *taille*. Indirect taxes, which were levied on the goods people bought rather than on their incomes, could be a greater burden than direct taxes and brought in more money for the Crown. They included the *gabelle* (a tax on salt) which varied enormously from one part of France to another, *aides* on food and drink and the *octrois* on goods entering towns.

The French monarchy never received enough money from taxes to cover its expenditure, so it frequently had to borrow. Borrowing was especially heavy in wartime, when government expenses increased dramatically. Interest payment on the debt became an increasingly large part of government expenditure in the eighteenth century.

The chaotic method of tax collection ensured that the government did not receive anything like the full amount of taxes which were levied. The Farmers-General was a company which collected the indirect taxes, paid an agreed lump sum to the government and kept for themselves anything above this, that they could collect. Direct taxes were collected by hundreds of accountants, who often used the money for their own purposes before passing it on to the King sometime later. The accountants had bought their positions (because of this these were known as 'venal' jobs) and could not be dismissed. This was because offices were regarded as a form of private property. On top of this, the lack of a central treasury into which all government revenues would be paid meant that the Controller-

General never knew in any particular year how much money there was to spend.

There were several checks on the King's power. The most important of these were the privileges of corporate bodies, like the provincial estates and the *parlements*. The *pays d'états* (provincial assemblies) like Brittany, were the last independent territories to be added to the French monarchy. They covered about half the kingdom and had ancient rights and privileges in justice and finance. They were exempt from paying some taxes. The provincial estates represented mainly the nobility and clung tenaciously to their privileges.

The *parlements* limited the King's powers. They were law-courts – final courts of appeal in their respective areas. There were 13 of them, of which the *Parlement* of Paris was by far the most important, as its jurisdiction covered about a third of France. The magistrates who sat in the courts were all *noblesse de robe* (so-called because of the robes officials wore), as their offices conferred noble status. Nearly all intendants and councillors of state and a majority of the King's ministers came from the *parlements*.) As the magistrates had bought their positions they could not be dismissed, unless the King repaid them the purchase price of their office.

In addition to their judicial functions, the *noblesse de robe* also had a political role. No law could be applied until it had been registered by each of the *parlements*. Before registering an edict the *parlement* could criticise it in a remonstrance sent to the King. If he wished, the King could ignore a remonstrance and insist, by what was known as a *lit de justice*, that the *parlement* register his edict. As the *parlements* opposed many of the royal edicts which aimed to change the system of taxation, they have been accused of defending their own privileges and selfish interests when they claimed to be representing the nation and opposing 'ministerial despotism'. They were seen as the main obstacle in the way of a reforming monarchy. A more sympathetic view of the *parlements* maintains that they were defending the law and the rights of the people against the authoritarian monarchy.

The *pays d'états* and the *parlements* were part of the administrative confusion which prevailed in France under the *ancien régime*. When kings created new structures they did not abolish the old ones. They simply added to them. In 1789 in France there were 35 provinces, 135 dioceses, 38 military regions and 34 *généralités*, as well as 13 *parlements*. None of these areas coincided with one another. There were different legal systems: Roman law in the south, various local laws in the north. France was also divided up into internal customs areas, so that goods moving from one part of France to another had to pay dues. There were various systems of weights and measures. There was therefore no uniform system of government which covered the whole of the country. This made it difficult for merchants and businessmen to conduct internal trade.

The character of the King was a factor in preventing reform. In

France the King alone had the power to carry through reforms, so if the old regime did not change it was the King's fault. Louis XVI was well-meaning and wanted to do what was best for France. He was a devout man and took seriously his duty, imposed by God, to rule in the interests of his subjects. Unfortunately, he lacked self-confidence and drive. 'The weakness and indecision of the King', wrote the Comte de Provence, the elder of his two brothers, 'are beyond description.' It was his need for an older figure on whom he could lean that led Louis, on ascending the throne at the age of 20 in 1774, to take Maurepas as his chief adviser. Maurepas was 73, had been out of office for 30 years and wanted a quiet life. He persuaded Louis to get rid of any minister who attempted reform or roused opposition. After Maurepas' death in 1781 Louis did not have a leading adviser and remained as indecisive as ever. He had little knowledge of the country over which he ruled, or of its people. Only once before the Revolution did he move outside the Paris-Versailles area, to inspect a new harbour at Cherbourg. Louis was a clumsy and awkward figure in public. He did not inspire respect, although most Frenchmen looked on him with affection up to 1789.

This could not be said of the Queen. Marie Antoinette, the daughter of the Habsburg Empress, Maria Theresa, was a symbol of the unpopular alliance with Austria which had led to France's defeat in the Seven Years War (1756–63). She had the determination that Louis lacked but she was regarded as frivolous and arrogant. In one year she ran up gambling debts of half a million *livres* and was known as Madame Deficit by her brother-in-law, the Comte de Provence. She was hated by nearly everyone.

3 The Enlightenment

> **KEY ISSUES** Who were the *philosophes*? In what ways did the enlightenment undermine royal government?

During the course of the eighteenth century there emerged in Europe an intellectual movement of writers and thinkers known as the enlightenment. The movement questioned and challenged a whole range of views and ideas which, at the time, were widely accepted – particularly relating to religion, nature and absolute monarchy. Their analysis was based on reason and rational thought, rather than superstition and tradition. In France the *philosophes* were writers rather than philosophers. The most famous of them were Voltaire, Montesquieu and Rousseau. They wrote on the problems of the day and attacked the prejudice and superstition they saw around them. Many of them contributed to the most important work of the French Enlightenment, The *Encyclopaedia* (edited by Diderot, the first volume of which appeared in 1752, the last of 35 in 1780). Their aim was to apply rational analysis to all activities. They were not prepared to accept tradition or revelation as a sufficient reason for doing anything. They were much more in favour of liberty – of the press, of speech, of trade, of freedom from arbitrary arrest – than of equality, although they did want equality before the law. The main objects of their attack were the Church and despotic government. They did not accept the literal interpretation of the Bible and rejected anything which could not be explained by reason – miracles, for example – as superstitious. They condemned the Catholic Church because it was wealthy, corrupt and intolerant. They took up Voltaire's cry of '*Écrasez l'infâme*' ('crush the infamous', meaning the Church).

The attack on despotism was mounted by Montesquieu in particular. His *Spirit of the Laws*, one of the most influential books in the eighteenth century, appeared in 1748. Monarchy, he said, was the government of one man according to the law, and despotism was the government of one man not restrained by law. It was arbitrary. Under it no-one could feel secure. Montesquieu had been president of the Parlement of Bordeaux and he saw the *parlements* and the provincial estates as having a special role as intermediaries between the King and his subjects. Their power prevented the King becoming a despot. Not surprisingly, the *parlements* were enthusiastic about his ideas, whilst public opinion largely accepted the *parlements* as defenders of the rights of the people against 'ministerial despotism'.

Rousseau, a citizen of Geneva who spent most of his life in France, was the writer who expressd the greatest sympathy with the people. He attacked the corruption of *ancien régime* society and shared a hostility to the established church and despotic government. In his *Social Contract* (1762) he developed the theory of popular sovereignty, whereby ordinary people would exercise political power.

The *philosophes* might criticise some institutions of the *ancien régime* but they were not opposed to the regime itself and they were not revolutionary. Many of them, including Montesquieu, were nobles and those who were not, like Voltaire and Rousseau, were accepted in high society.

What impact if any, did the writings of the *philosophes* have on the outbreak of the revolution? Although the *philosophes* were not revolutionary the effect of their teaching was, as they attacked all the assumptions on which the *ancien régime* rested. They challenged, and in particular, helped to undermine the unity of the *ancien régime* by questioning and attacking its key pillars, namely the position of the church and the role of the King as God's servant. By the 1780s much of France, at all social levels, was prepared for widespread changes and eager to bring them about. The Comte de Ségur commented:

i We lent enthusiastic support to the philosophic doctrines professed by bold and witty scribblers. Voltaire won us over, Rousseau touched our hearts and we felt a secret pleasure when we saw them attack an old

structure that appeared to us gothic [harsh] and ridiculous. So what-
5 ever our rank, our privileges, the remains of our former power eaten
away beneath our feet, we enjoyed this little war. Untouched by it, we
were mere onlookers. These battles . . . did not seem to us likely to
affect the worldly superiority we enjoyed and which centuries-old professions made us believe indestructible . . . It can be pleasurable to sink
10 so long as one believes one can rise again at will.

The ideas of Montesquieu were expressed in the remonstrances of
the *parlements*. The French historian Chaussinand-Nogaret found that
the *cahiers* (list of grievances) of the nobles in 1789 were steeped in
the ideas of the Enlightenment. Their authors were deeply hostile to
the *ancien régime* and anxious to create a state that was liberal and representative.

On the other hand, the American historian G.V. Taylor did not
find much influence of the Enlightenment in the *cahiers* of the Third
Estate, which were very conservative. 'The only possible conclusion',
he wrote, 'is that the revolutionary programme and its ideology were
produced and perfected after the voters had deliberated in the spring
[of 1789] and that the great majority of them neither foresaw nor
intended what was about to be done'. Other historians have followed
this line of thinking in maintaining that the influence of the
Enlightenment came after the Revolution had begun and not before
it. Only when the *ancien régime* had collapsed and new institutions had
to be constructed did the ideas of the Enlightenment produce a revolutionary ideology.

4 French Society

> **KEY ISSUE** How was French society organised during the *ancien*
> *régime?*

French society in the eighteenth century was divided into orders
or Estates. The First Estate was the clergy, the Second Estate was
the nobility and the Third Estate was the rest of the population,
made up of bourgeoisie (the wealthy middle class), peasants and
urban workers.

a) The First Estate

There were about 130,000 clergy. Of these 60,000 were members of
religious orders (monks and nuns). The 70,000 secular clergy worked
in the parishes. It was common for the younger sons (the eldest son
inherited everything from his father, younger sons had to provide for
themselves) of the great noble families to enter the higher posts in
the Church, so they could enjoy its vast wealth.The Archbishopric of
Strasbourg received over 400,000 *livres* per annum (most *curés*, parish

priests, received between 700 and 1,000 *livres* per annum). Many bishops held more than one bishopric and never appeared in their dioceses at all. This was one of the great scandals which made the Church so unpopular.

The wealth of the Church came from the land it owned and from the tithes. It was the single largest landowner in France, owning about ten per cent of the land, although the proportion varied greatly from one area to another. In the north the Church held up to a third of the land, while in Auverque it held only three per cent. The tithe was a proportion of the each year's crop paid to the Church by landowners. Here again there was no uniformity. In parts of Dauphiné it was not much of a burden, as it amounted to only one fiftieth of the crop, but in Brittany it was as much as a quarter. In most of France it was about seven to eight per cent of the crop. The tithe was supposed to provide for the local priest, poor relief and the upkeep of the church building, but most of it went instead to the bishops and abbots. This was greatly resented, by both lower clergy and peasants, as their *cahiers* showed in 1789.

The Church had many privileges apart from collecting the tithe. Its most important privilege and one which added to its unpopularity was its exemption from taxation. Instead of paying taxes, the Assembly of the Clergy, dominated by the bishops, negotiated with the King to make an annual payment to the Crown, known as a *don gratuit* or 'free gift'. It was always much less than they would have paid in normal taxation and was under five per cent of clerical income.

Catholicism was the state religion, yet the functions of the Church extended far beyond the practice of religion. It had wide-ranging powers of censorship, provided poor relief, hospitals and schools and kept a list in the parish registers of all births, marriages and deaths. It also acted as a sort of Ministry of Information, as the only way government policies became widely known was through the priests informing their congregations.

b) The Second Estate

The Second Estate was the most powerful. There have been widely differing estimates of the number of nobles, including their families, which range from 110,000 to 350,000 – between 0.5 per cent and 1.5 per cent of the population. Even if the lowest figure of 25,000 families is taken, this is over a hundred times larger than the British peerage (220 in 1790). The most powerful were the 4,000 court nobility, restricted in theory to those whose noble ancestry went back before 1400; in practice to those who could afford the high cost of living at Versailles. Second in political importance were the *noblesse de robe*, the legal and administrative nobles, especially the 1,200 magistrates of the *parlements*. The rest of the nobles, the majority, had never seen Versailles and lived in the country. Landed estates were inherited by the oldest son (according to the law of primogeniture), other sons, who also inherited noble status, had to find jobs in the Church, the army or the administration. Buying an office was expensive and about a quarter of the nobility were too poor to do so. They had, therefore, either to enlist in the army or work their small estates themselves.

The main source of income for the Second Estate was land. The nobility owned between a quarter and a third of the land in France and between 15 per cent and 25 per cent of the Church's income went to them, as all the bishops were nobles. Nearly all the highest positions in the land were held by nobles. They were the King's ministers, his high legal officials, his *intendants* in the provinces, and they occupied all the highest ranks in the army. In his pamphlet 'What is the Third Estate?' The Abbé Sieyès wrote in 1789:

1   In one way or another, all the branches of the executive have been taken over by the caste [class] that monopolises the Church, the judiciary and the army. A spirit of fellowship leads the nobles to favour one another over the rest of the nation. Their domination is complete;
5   they truly reign.

In addition to holding all the top jobs, nobles enjoyed many privileges. They were tried in special courts, and were exempt from military service, the *gabelle* and the *corvée* (forced labour on the roads). They received feudal (also known as seigneurial) dues (see page 12), had exclusive rights to hunting and fishing and in many areas the monopoly right (known as *banalités*) to operate mills, ovens and winepresses. They also benefited from tax exemptions. Until 1695 they did not pay direct taxes at all. Then the *capitation* was introduced and in 1749 the *vingtième*, though they managed to pay less than they should have done of these taxes. They were generally exempt from the most onerous tax of all, the *taille*. The provincial nobles were strongly attached to these privileges, as the loss of feudal dues could lead to a drop in their income of as much as 60 per cent in areas such as Upper Brittany (the loss in other areas could be as little as 10 per cent). It was the less wealthy of the nobles who felt that if they were to lose their tax privileges and give up their seigneurial rights they would be ruined. They opposed change and clung to their privileges, as these were all they had to distinguish them from commoners.

Historians before the 1960s talked of an 'aristocratic reaction', when nobles sought to prevent the bourgeoisie from becoming enobled and acquiring high positions in the State. The 'Ségur Ordinance' of 1781, stated that no-one could become an officer in the army unless his family had been ennobled for four generations, has been produced as evidence for this. Yet the Ordinance was intended to help the poor provincial nobility, for whom the army was the main source of employment, against the rich *anoblis* (those recently ennobled) who had been able to buy promotion in the army. It was a struggle between the rich and the poor members of the nobility. There were no signs in the late eighteenth century that the nobility was becoming a closed group. It was possible to become a noble either by direct grant of the King or by buying certain offices. There were 50,000 of these venal offices in the royal civil service which could be bought, sold and inherited like any other property. 12,000 of these were ennobling offices. In the eighteenth century 2,200 families were ennobled by buying offices and 4,300 by the direct grant of the King. Thus between a quarter and a third of all noble families in 1789 had been recently ennobled. The nobility was an open élite. Turgot recognised this in 1776 when he wrote about the ease with which nobility could be purchased:

> There is no rich man who does not immediately become noble and as a result the body of noblemen includes all the rich men and the controversy over privileges is no longer a matter of distinguished families against commoners but a matter of rich against poor.

The idea of an 'aristocratic reaction' stems from the belief that the economic strength of the nobles was declining, compared with that of the economically dominant bourgeoisie. Although nobles would suffer derogation (loss of their nobility) if they took part in the activities of commoners such as retail trade or manual work, iron-founding and mining were excluded from this ban. Nobles were involved in industries such as mining and metallurgy and were also major investors in trading companies (wholesale trade) and banking. As landlords they benefited from the rise of rents, which increased in the late eighteenth century as a result of population pressure. The American historian Robert Forster has shown that the richest people in the Toulouse area were 20 noble families, who doubled their income from land in the second half of the century. In Paris in 1749 nearly all the people with an income of over half a million *livres* were nobles. Even in industrial centres such as Lyon nobles remained the wealthiest group. Only in the thriving seaports on the Atlantic, such as Bordeaux, were the bourgeoisie wealthier than the local nobles and here the richest moved up into the ranks of the nobility.

c) The Third Estate

The third estate consisted of everyone who did not belong to one or other of the two privileged estates. There were enormous extremes of wealth within this estate. At the top end were the rich merchants, industrialists and business people. This group, rich commoners who were not peasants or urban workers, is frequently called the bourgeoisie. Some bourgeois were involved in industry, most were not. Among the wealthiest bourgeoisie were merchants, as French overseas trade was the most dynamic sector of the economy, with the volume of trade increasing by 440 per cent between 1715 and 1789. Other bourgeois were financiers, landowners, members of the liberal professions (such as doctors and writers), lawyers and civil servants, many of whom were venal office-holders. The bourgeoisie owned 39,000 out of the 50,000 venal offices. There were about 2.3 million bourgeoisie in 1789 (just over eight per cent of the population). This was a threefold increase since 1700.

Historians who regarded the nobility as declining in wealth, saw the bourgeoisie as rising in status and anxious to gain political power. As noble privilege stood in the way, the bourgeoisie was considered as being hostile to the nobility. This is not entirely accurate. The bourgeoisie were certainly rising in the eighteenth century, not only in numbers but also in wealth. Finance, industry and banking accounted for 20 per cent of French private wealth in the 1780s and of this the bourgeoisie had a large share. Vast fortunes were made in the Atlantic ports of Bordeaux, La Rochelle and Nantes by the colonial trade with the West Indies. The remaining 80 per cent of French wealth came largely from *rentes* (interest from investments in government stock) and income from the land. The bourgeoisie held about a quarter of the land in France and often owned seigneurial rights too, as they were a form of property that could be bought by anyone. About 15 per cent of *seigneurs* were bourgeois.

Although the bourgeoisie were rising, they were not opposed to the nobility and did not question the system of privileges, at least until 1788. They accepted noble values as their own and wished to share in the system of privilege by becoming ennobled. The *avocats* (lawyers) of Nuits in Burgundy declared as late as December, 1788:

> The privileges of the nobility are truly their property. We will respect them all the more because we are not excluded from them and can acquire them . . . Why, then . . . think of destroying the source of emulation [inspiration] which guides our labours?

Most ennobling offices required two or three generations of holders before hereditary nobility was acquired. However, this delay could be avoided by the very wealthy. The slave trader, planter or financier could afford the high cost of an office such as King's Secretary, which conferred hereditary nobility directly. The merchants who made vast fortunes copied the nobility by abandoning trade as soon as possible and put their money into land, office or *rentes*, as trade was regarded as ignoble and dishonourable. Bourgeoisie and nobles became part of a single, propertied élite. There was little bourgeois hostility to the nobility before 1788.

If the bourgeoisie was by far the wealthiest part of the Third Estate, at the other extreme was the peasantry. They were by far the most numerous section of society. About 85 per cent of the French population lived in the countryside and most of them were peasants. Estimates of the amount of the land they owned vary from 25–45 per cent of the total, though these figures disguise wide regional differences. There was a small group (perhaps 600,000) of large-scale farmers who grew for the market, employed other peasants as day labourers and loaned money. More numerous were the *laboureurs*, peasants who grew enough food to feed themselves and in a good year had a small surplus. For most of the eighteenth century they, and the big farmers, did well, as there were boom conditions until the 1770s. Although the majority of peasants had some land, it was not enough to live on. In order to survive they worked as day labourers and wove cloth in their homes. Half the peasants were share-croppers, who had no capital and gave half their produce to their landlords. About a quarter of all peasants were landless labourers, who owned nothing but their house and garden. Serfdom continued to exist in France. There were still a million serfs in the east, mainly in Franche Comté. Their children could not inherit even their personal property without paying considerable dues to their lord. The poor peasant had no hope of improvement and lived in a chronic state of uncertainty. Bad weather or illness could push him into the ranks of the vagrants, who lived by begging, stealing and occasional employment.

All peasants had to pay tithe to the Church, taxes to the State and feudal dues to their lord. In the eighteenth century 'feudalism' meant the rights and privileges enjoyed by landlords and the dues and obligations owed to them by peasants. Nearly all land was subject to feudal dues. These included the *corvée, champart*, harvest dues and *lods et ventes* (a payment to the *seigneur* when property changes hands). A further grievance was that the peasant could be tried in the seigneurial court, where the lord acted as judge and jury. The incidence of all these dues varied considerably from one part of France to another. Peasants in the Midi paid hardly any feudal dues, whereas in Brittany and Burgundy they were heavy.

Taxes paid to the State included the *taille, vingtième, capitation* and *gabelle*. All these increased enormously between 1749 and the 1780s, in order to pay for the wars in which France became involved. Taxes took between five and ten per cent of the peasants' income.

The heaviest burden on the peasants was often not taxes, the tithe or feudal dues, but rents. These increased markedly in the second half of the eighteenth century as a result of the increase in population, which is estimated to have risen from 22.4 million in 1705 to 27.9 million in 1790. This increased the demand for farms, with the result that landlords could raise rents.

The third part of the Third Estate was made up of urban workers. Small property owners and artisans in Paris were known as *sans-culottes*, because they wore trousers rather than breeches. The majority of workers in the towns lived in crowded and insanitary tenements. They were unskilled and poor. Skilled craftsmen were

A contemporary cartoon showing a peasant crushed by the weight of taxes and dues such as the *taille* and the *corvée*, imposed by the privileged first and second estates.

organised in guilds. In Paris in 1776 they had 100,000 members, a third of the male population. Working hours were long – in busy times, typically, sixteen hours a day, six days a week. Workers were not allowed to combine to obtain higher wages or better working conditions. The standard of living of wage-earners had slowly fallen in the eighteenth century, as prices had risen on average by 65 per cent between 1726 and 1789, wages by only 22 per cent.

There was scarcely any large-scale production: the average number of people in the workshops of Paris in 1789 was 16. Masters and men worked and lived together and both were affected by a rise in the price of bread after a bad harvest, as bread formed three-quarters of most workers' diet. When prices rose they tended to seek a reduction in the price of bread rather than a rise in wages. Like the peasant in the countryside, they seized supplies in times of shortage and sold them at a 'fair' price.

References

1 Roland Mousnier, *The Assassination of Henry IV*, (London, 1973), pp. 50–52.
2 The decision to abolish torture was taken by the government of Louis XVI.
3 R. Sharrock, *Selected Poems of W. Wordsworth* (London, 1958) p. 23.

Working on Chapter 1

Now that you have read this chapter you will hopefully be familiar with the structure of French society during the *ancien régime* and the main problems which faced the King's government in the years before the revolution. Although you are unlikely to be asked a direct question on the *ancien régime*, a knowledge of it, is essential when you write about the origins of the French Revolution. To be certain that you understand the background, you may well find it useful to make notes on:

a) The main problems which faced the King before 1789
b) The impact which the *philosophes* of the enlightenment had on the origin of the French revolution

Answering source and structured questions on Chapter 1

1 The Enlightenment
Read carefully the account by the Comte de Ségur on pages 6–7. Answer the following questions:

a) Why do you think he 'lent enthusiastic support to the philosophic doctrines' (line 1)? (*4 marks*)
b) What indications are there in what he says that he would be likely to regret his 'support'? (*6 marks*)
c) Does the cartoon (page 13) and other extracts in the chapter, support or contradict what Ségur says? Explain your answer. (*10 marks*)

2 The King's Government and French Society
a) Explain the main problems facing French society during the *ancien régime*. (*8 marks*)
b) To what extent was the power of the King limited before the revolution? (*12 marks*)

2 The Origins of the French Revolution

POINTS TO CONSIDER

Why the French Revolution occurred is one of the central issues in this book and one of the most studied topics in European history. You will need to consider carefully how a number of long standing and deep rooted problems relating to finance and government came to a head during the years 1788 – 9. An important issue is why attempts at reform failed, and with such spectacular consequences for the crown and the nation? How did a revolt of the nobility lead to a wholesale assault on the structure of the *ancien régime*? As you read the chapter for the first time note how the pace and momentum of change quickened by the summer of 1789.

KEY DATES

1614 Last summoning of the Estates General before 1789
1756 Start of the Seven Years War
1774 Accession of Louis XVI
1778 France entered the American War of Independence
1781 Necker published his *Compte Rendu au Roi*
1787 Assembly of Notables met; Louis' reform package rejected.
1789 Feb Sieyès published the pamphlet '*What is the Third Estate?*'
      May Estates general met at Versailles
      June National Assembly proclaimed
      June Tennis Court Oath
      July The storming of the Bastille
      Aug Decrees dismantling feudalism passed

1 Introduction

KEY ISSUE What are the various movements in the opening phase of the revolution?

Georges Lefebvre[1] saw in the years 1787–9 not one revolutionary movement but four. First came the revolution of the aristocracy, which sought to defend its privileges and even extend them. Through the *parlements* and the Assembly of Notables, it resisted attempts by the Crown to reduce its taxation privileges. It was the aristocracy who demanded the calling of the Estates-General and it was this that led to the second revolution, that of the bourgeoisie. The bourgeoisie had supported the aristocracy in its opposition to 'ministerial despotism' until September 1788, when the *Parlement* of Paris said that the Estates-General should be formed as it was when it last met in 1614.

This would mean that the two privileged orders would be able to out-vote the Third Estate. The bourgeois leaders of the Third Estate would not accept this and so began a struggle against the aristocracy. They sought equality and this involved destroying the privileges of the nobility and the Church and setting up a system where promotion to high office was according to merit, not birth, where all paid taxes on the same basis and where the law was the same for all. The Revolution of 1789 was, above all else, the struggle for equal rights.

In its struggle against the King and the privileged orders – for the two had now combined to resist the bourgeois assault – the bourgeoisie needed the support of the Paris populace. In July the Crown attempted to use force to dissolve the National Assembly but was prevented from doing so by the rising of the *menu peuple*, the artisans and workers of Paris, which culminated in the fall of the Bastille. This saved the National Assembly and ensured the success of the Revolution. This third revolution, the popular revolution, arose from the economic crisis which had seen the price of bread rise to its highest point on the day the Bastille fell, 14 July 1789. Meanwhile, a fourth revolution, that of the peasants, was taking place. This had begun in the spring of 1789 and sought the abolition of seigneurial dues and labour services. Like the popular revolt, the peasant revolution resulted from the economic crisis and the bad harvest of 1788.

2 The Financial Crisis

KEY ISSUE What was the nature and extent of the financial crisis?

The most important of the immediate causes of the French Revolution was the financial deficit that was being amassed by the State. On 20 August 1786, Calonne, the Controller-General, told Louis XVI that the government was on the verge of bankruptcy. Revenue for 1786 would be 475 million livres, while expenditure would be 587 million livres, making a deficit of 112 million – almost a quarter of the total income. A much more detailed and alarming picture of the situation is provided in the Treasury Account of 1788, which has been called the first and last budget of the monarchy. The Account reveals that in 1788 Government expenditure totalled more than 629 livres, against an income of 503 million livres. The deficit had increased in two years to 126 million – 20 per cent of total expenditure. Out of total expenditure, the government allocated 12 million (under 2 per cent of the total) to public education and poor relief, 165 million (26 per cent of the total) to the military, but the debt obligation consumed a massive 318 million livres (over 50 per cent of the budget).[2] It was anticipated that for 1789, receipts would amount to only 325 million livres and that interest payment on the deficit would amount to 62 per cent of the receipts.

Why was there a deficit and a financial crisis in France? Two factors are significant in helping to explain this. Firstly, between 1740 and 1783, France was at war for 20 years, first in the War of the Austrian Succession (1740–48), then the Seven Years War (1756–63) and finally the American War of Independence (1778–83). It has been estimated that the cost of helping the American colonists defeat the British government was approximately 1,066 million livres.[3] This was mainly financed by loans, and in itself did not necessarily lead to revolution. Britain was also heavily in debt and her tax burden per head was three times heavier than in France. The difference was that in Britain Parliament guaranteed loans, whereas in France there was no such representative body to give confidence to lenders.

Secondly, the Crown was not receiving much of the money collected in taxes (see page 3), and until it recovered control of its finances, no basic reforms could be carried out. The privileged classes, whose incomes from property had increased, were an untapped source of revenue which the crown needed to access. There would be powerful resistance to any change in the taxation structure from those with a vested interest in retaining the status quo.

3 Attempts at Reform

> **KEY ISSUE** Why did attempts at reform fail?

During the American War Jacques Necker, Director-General of Finance, obtained loans to pay for French involvement. He was very successful, raising 520 million livres between 1777 and his resignation in May 1781. However, in order to persuade financiers to lend, he had to pay a very high rate of interest. This increased the Crown's debts enormously. Necker was a controversial figure. He did attempt to tackle the problem of gaining control over financial administration by seeking to replace the independent, venal financiers by salaried officials, whom the Controller General could appoint and dismiss. He succeeded in getting rid of 50 of the most powerful Receivers-General (accountants). He also took steps to establish a central Treasury, into which all taxes would be paid and from which all expenditures would be made.

In 1781 he issued the *Compte Rendu* to assure creditors that the interest on their loans was secure. This was the first public statement of the royal finances and it created a sensation. It carefully distinguished between ordinary peacetime expenditure and extraordinary wartime costs. Necker showed that there was a surplus of 10 million livres on the ordinary account. When he tried to bring the biggest spenders, the Ministers of War and the Marine, under his control and demanded a seat on the royal council, the other ministers threatened to resign. The King failed to support his reforming minister and Necker was dismissed. In many ways Necker did a disservice to the crown and future Controllers-General by achieving the seemingly impossible, namely financing a successful war without raising any new taxes, and providing to the nation for the first time ever the state of the Kingdom's finances, which remarkably showed a surplus.

Necker's successor, Joly de Fleury, discovered the true nature of France's finances. The Treasury was 160 million livres short for 1781 and 295 million livres short for 1782.[4] To make good the shortfall Fleury, and especially Calonne who followed him, undid much of Necker's work by resuming the practice of selling offices (many of which Necker had abolished). Both Fleury and Calonne borrowed much more heavily than Necker had done. Calonne had to offer 12–16 per cent interest to attract loans, as by the 1780s Britain, America and Russia were regarded as more secure places for investment than France. In 1786, with loans drying up, Calonne was forced to grasp the nettle and embark upon a reform of the tax system. His plan consisted of an ambitious three part programme. The main proposal was to replace the *capitation* and *vingtième* on landed property, by a single land tax. It was to have been a tax on the land and not a tax on the person, and would therefore affect all landed property – church, noble and common alike, regardless of whether the lands were used for luxury purposes or crops. There were to be no exemptions, everyone including the nobles, the clergy and the *pays d'états* would pay. The second part of his programme was aimed at economic stimulation to ensure that future tax revenues would increase. In order to try to achieve this he proposed abandoning controls on the grain trade and abolishing internal customs barriers. The final part of the programme was to try to restore national confidence so that new loans for the short term could be raised. He also hoped that by doing this the *parlements* would be less likely to oppose the registration of his measures. He hoped to achieve this by some display of national consensus.

The obvious body to summon was the Estates–General, but this was rejected as being too unpredictable. He opted instead for an Assembly of Notables. In a Memorandum to Louis XVI (August 1786), Calonne noted that '. . . with Assemblies of Notables the King individually summons those whom he sees fit'. The hope and expectation was that a docile and pliant body would be chosen, which would then meekly agree to the reform programme. Calonne's plan failed. He misjudged the situation. The 144 members of the Assembly met, after some delay, in February 1787. It included leading members of the *parlements*, princes, leading nobles and important bishops. Some were personally opposed to Calonne. Once they had an opportunity to examine the proposals it became clear they would not be willing collaborators in the reform process. As representatives

A Contemporary French cartoon depicting the Assembly of Notables as birds. President Monkey (Calonne) addresses the Notables and asks them with which sauce they would like to be eaten

of the privileges orders, with most to lose from the reforms, they immediately attacked and rejected Calonne's proposals. The Notables were not opposed to all change. They agreed that taxation should be on an equal basis, but they claimed that the approval of the nation was needed for Calonne's reforms and called for a meeting of the Estates-General, which had last met in 1614. Louis, realising the strength of opposition to Calonne, dismissed him in April 1787.

In calling the Notables, the King had appeared to admit that he needed the consent of a national assembly for his reforms. Public opinion supported the Notables, who were seen as opponents of royal despotism. At this stage everyone seemed to be opposed to the King and his ministers. Louis' failure to support Calonne was an indication of his own indecisiveness in the rapidly escalating crisis.

Calonne was replaced by one of the Notables, Loménie de Brienne, Archbishop of Toulouse, whilst another Notable,

Lamoignon, President of the *Parlement* of Paris, became head of the Judiciary. As the Assembly of Notables was no more co-operative with Brienne than it had been with Calonne, its session was ended on 25 May. Brienne, retained Calonne's land tax but also took up Necker's work and began an extensive programme of reform. There was to be an end to venal financial officials, a new central treasury established, laws codified, the educational system reformed, religious toleration introduced and the army made more efficient and less expensive. But Brienne now had to put his reforms before the *Parlement* of Paris for registration. The *Parlement* refused registration and said that only the Estates-General could consent to new taxes. The popularity of the monarchy was declining rapidly, especially when the King exiled the *Parlement* to Troyes on 15 August.

The opposition of the Paris and provincial *parlements* paralysed the government because it prevented the Crown from obtaining the money it needed. As a result, the King gave way and in September allowed the *Parlement* to return to Paris. New taxation was abandoned and Brienne agreed to call the Estates-General before 1792. Arthur Young was acutely aware of the prevailing anxiety and confusion when he dined in Paris in October 1787:

1 One opinion pervaded the whole company, that they are on the eve of some great revolution [i.e. change] in the government: that everything points to it: the confusion in the finances great; with a deficit impossible to provide for without the states-general of the kingdom,
5 yet no ideas formed of what would be the consequence of their meeting . . . a great ferment amongst all ranks of men, who are eager for some change, without knowing what to look to, or to hope for: and a strong leaven of liberty, increasing every hour since the American revolution; . . . it is very remarkable that such conversation never occurs
10 but a bankruptcy is a topic: the curious question on which is, would a bankruptcy occasion a civil war and a total overthrow of the government?

On 3 May 1788 the *Parlement* appeared as the defender of the rights of the nation in proclaiming the 'fundamental laws' of the kingdom. It said that the right to vote taxes belonged solely to the Estates-General, that Frenchmen could not be imprisoned without trial and that the King could not change the privileges and customs of the provinces. As a result, Lamoignon decided to curtail drastically the powers of the *Parlement*. On 8 May 1788 the *parlements* were deprived of their right to register, and protest against, royal decrees. This would now be carried out by a new Plenary Court, whose members would be appointed by the King. The judicial powers of the *Parlement* were also reduced. Much of their work was given to other courts. It appeared to many observers that ministerial despotism had returned. Attempts at reform were not succeeding. Alexis de Tocquevile writing in the middle of the nineteenth century summed up the situation when he noted that the most dangerous moment for a bad government is when it begins to reform itself. He suggested that it was not so much the absence of reform that was the problem, but its nature. In opening the eyes of the population to better things it seemed to speed up the drive towards revolution rather than prevent it.[5]

4 The Aristocratic Revolt

> **KEY ISSUES** Why did the French aristocracy revolt? How serious was the opposition?

The result of the King's high-handed action was an aristocratic revolt: the most violent opposition that the government had yet met. There were riots in some of the provincial capitals where the *parlements* met, such as Rennes in Brittany and Grenoble in Dauphiné. In all parts of the country nobles met in unauthorised assemblies to discuss action in favour of the *parlements*. An Assembly of the Clergy also joined in on the side of the *parlements*, breaking its long tradition of loyalty to the Crown. It condemned the reforms and voted a *don gratuit* of less than a quarter the size requested by the Crown.

How serious was all this opposition? It was restricted to a few places, which were far from Paris and from each other. The actions of those protesting were unco-ordinated. In Paris there was no popular support for the nobles' revolt. Had they been given time, the new courts would probably have worked efficiently. It was likely that the trouble would have passed away, as it had done in the early 1770s, when the *Parlement* of Paris had been exiled and new courts set up.

What prevented this from happening was the collapse of the government's finances. Financiers were no longer willing to lend money to the government, owing to the economic crisis and Lamoignon's May edicts. At the beginning of August 1788 the royal treasury was empty. Brienne agreed that the Estates-General should meet on 1 May 1789 and he suspended payments from the royal treasury – the Crown was bankrupt. He realised that only one man could restore government credit and so he persuaded the King, who was reluctant, to recall Necker. Brienne then resigned, as did Lamoignon. Necker returned to office and made it clear that, apart from raising loans to allow the government to function, he would do nothing until the Estates-General had met. He abandoned the reforms of Lamoignon and recalled the *Parlement*. The King had been compelled to abandon the reforms of his ministers and to accept the calling of a representative body, the Estates-General. In 1787 the then navy minister, the Marquis de Castries, had perceptively told the King, 'As a Frenchman

I want the Estates-General, as a minister I am bound to tell you that they might destroy your authority'.

5 The Estates-General

> **KEY ISSUE** How did the Estates-General become the National Assembly?

When the Paris *Parlement* returned in September and declared that the Estates-General should meet as in 1614 it lost its popularity overnight. Up to this point the bourgeoisie had taken little part in political agitation, which had been led by the privileged classes – the nobles and the clergy in the *Parlement* and the Assembly of Notables. Now the bourgeois leaders of the Third Estate began to suspect that the privileged orders had opposed 'ministerial despotism' because they wanted power for themselves and not because they wanted justice for the nation as a whole. They now demanded double representation for the Third Estate (so that they would have as many representatives as the other two orders combined), and voting by head instead of by order. They knew that this would give them a majority, as many of the First Estate, who were poor parish priests, would support the Third Estate. A Swiss observer, Mallet du Pan, wrote:

> Public debate has assumed a different character. King, despotism and constitution have become only secondary questions. Now it is war between the Third Estate and the other two orders.

This hostility was reflected in a pamphlet 'What is the Third Estate?', written by the Abbé Sieyès and published in January 1789. In this he attacked the First and Second Estates, not royal despotism. He said that if the privileged orders refused to join the Third Estate in a common assembly, then the commons, who represented the overwhelming majority of the nation, should take direction of the nation's affairs into its own hands.

In December 1788 the King's Council allowed the doubling of Third Estate deputies. Nothing was said about voting by head, so that when the Estates-General met there was bound to be confusion, the Third Estate assuming that there would be voting by head (otherwise doubling served no purpose), while the first two Estates assumed that there would not.

All the adult male members of the two privileged orders had a vote for electing their deputies. The Third Estate were to be chosen by a complicated system of indirect election. Frenchmen over the age of 25 could vote in their primary assembly, either of their parish or their urban guild, if they paid taxes. They chose representatives who in turn elected the deputies.

Before the meeting of the Estates-General the electors of each of the three orders drew up *cahiers*, lists of grievances and suggestions for reform. Those of the First Estate reflected the interests of the parish clergy. They called for an end to bishops holding more than one diocese, and for those who were not noble to be able to become bishops. In return they were prepared to give up the financial privileges of the Church. They were not, however, prepared to give up the dominant position of the Church: Catholicism should remain the established religion and retain control of education. They did not intend to tolerate Protestantism.

The noble *cahiers* were surprisingly liberal – 89 per cent were prepared to give up their financial privileges and nearly 39 per cent supported voting by head, at least on matters of general interest. Instead of trying to preserve their own privileges, they showed a desire for change and were prepared to admit that merit rather than birth should be the key to high office. They attacked the government for its despotism, its inefficiency and its injustice. On many issues they were more liberal than the Third Estate.

Parish *cahiers* of the Third Estate reflected the wishes of the peasants. The following extract from the *cahier* sent by the village of Le Revest is a typical example:

1   Placed on an arid soil, shakled and confined by the bonds of feudalism, confused in the maze of laws, exhausted by the multiplicity of tribunals of appeal, our most constant labours and bitter privations hardly provide us with the means of meeting the charges of the State and the
5   Province. The tithe adds to these burdens and its charges form a load under which we remain crushed. The best of Kings can hear us; (a reference to the peasants belief that Louis was willing to help them) he will lighten our lot to attain this end. The deputies who will be elected to represent the Third Order at the Estates General will be expressly
10   instructed to petition for the reform of the civil and criminal code; the obligation of magistrates to judge according to the letter of the law. They will request the right to qualify for all military posts, honours and pensions confined to the nobility; that no exemptions can be accorded from the payment of any dues and impositions due to the king. They will
15   request also a deduction in the price of salt, to make it uniform throughout the kingdom; give us the power to grow tobacco on our land. The right of the third estate to have as many members as the first two orders combined. A general tax upon all property to be collected in the same manner and form; the sending of money due to the king
20   directly from the Province to the treasury of the state.

The *cahiers* of all three orders had a great deal in common. All were against absolute royal power and all wanted a King whose powers would be limited by an elected assembly, which would have the right to vote taxes and pass laws. Only one major issue separated the Third Estate from the other two orders – voting by head. It was this that was to cause conflict when the Estates-General met.

The government did not make any attempt to influence the elections to the Estates-General and had no candidates. The clergy overwhelmingly elected parish priests: only 51 of the 303 deputies were bishops. The majority of noble deputies were from old noble families in the provinces, many of them poor and conservative, but 90 out of the 282 could be classed as liberals and these were to play a leading role in the Estate-General. The 610 deputies elected to represent the Third Estate were educated, articulate and almost entirely well-off, largely because deputies were expected to pay their own expenses. This was something peasants and artisans could not afford. Not a single peasant or urban worker was elected. The largest group of Third Estate deputies were venal office holders (43 per cent), followed by lawyers (25 per cent), although two-thirds of deputies had some legal qualification. Only 13 per cent were from trade and industry. The industrial middle class did not play a leading role in events leading to the Revolution or, indeed, in the Revolution itself.

When the Estates-General met on 5 May 1789 the government had the opportunity to take control of the situation. The Third Estate deputies, lacking experience and having no recognised leaders, would have supported the King if he had promised reforms, but the government did not take the initiative and it put forward no programme. Necker talked about equality of taxation but did not mention any other reform. Nothing was said about a constitution which would set out how France was to be governed, which all the *cahiers* had demanded.

Although the Estates-General met in three separate groups, the Third Estate insisted that the credentials of those who claimed to have been elected should be verified in a common session. This appeared a trivial matter but was seen by everyone as deciding whether the Estates-General should meet as one body (and vote by head) when discussing all other matters. The nobles rejected the Third Estate's demand and declared themselves a separate order by 188 votes to 46, as did the clergy but with a slender majority of 19. The Third Estate refused to do anything until the other two orders joined them, so weeks of paralysis followed, with the government failing to provide any leadership. Finally, on 10 June, the deadlock was broken when the Third Estate passed a motion that verification should begin, even if the other two orders did not accept their invitation to verify credentials in common. A trickle of priests joined the Third Estate in the following days, which in 17 June voted by 491 to 90 to call itself the National Assembly. The Third Estate was now claiming that, as it represented most of the nation, it had the right to manage its affairs and decide taxation. Events were rapidly moving out of the control of the government, especially when on 19 June the clergy voted to join the Third Estate.

All of this was a direct challenge to the authority of the King, who was at last forced to act. He decided to hold a Royal Session, attended by all three Estates, on 23 June, when he would propose a series of reforms. On 20 June the deputies of the Third Estate found that the hall in which they met had been closed to prepare for the Royal Session. They had not been informed and were furious. They met instead on a tennis court nearby and took an oath, known as the Tennis Court Oath, not to disperse until they had given France a constitution, thus claiming that the King had not the right to dissolve them. Only one member voted against the motion; 90 had voted against a motion to call themselves the National Assembly only three days before, so the deputies were rapidly becoming more radical.

It was Necker's idea to hold a Royal Session, where he hoped the King would ignore the events of 10–17 June and would accept voting in common on all important matters. Louis, under pressure from the Queen and his brothers, ignored this advice and came down very firmly on the side of the privileged orders. He declared null and void the decisions taken by the deputies of the Third Estate on 17 June. He would not allow the privileges of the nobility and clergy to be discussed in common. However, he was prepared to accept considerable restrictions on his own power. No taxes would be imposed 'without the consent of the representatives of the nation', *lettres de cachet* would be abolished and freedom of the press introduced. Internal customs barriers, the *gabelle* and *corvée* were to be abolished. If these reforms had been put forward in May, a majority of the Third Estate would probably have been satisfied but now they did not go far enough. The King ended by ordering the deputies to disperse and meet in their separate assemblies.

The next day 151 clergy joined the Third Estate. The day after that 47 nobles, including a royal prince (the Duc d'Orléans), did the same. There were popular demonstrations in Paris in favour of the Assembly. On 27 June the King gave way. He reversed his decision of 23 June and ordered the nobles and clergy to join the Third Estate and vote by head. Arthur Young wrote on the 27th: 'The whole business now seems over and the revolution complete'. There was rejoicing in Paris.

Was the King prepared to accept what had happened or was he simply trying to buy time, so that he could call up troops to crush the Assembly? He had given the first orders to bring up troops to Paris and Versailles on 22 June. By late June nearly 4,000 troops, including 2,600 in foreign-speaking units, were stationed round Paris. This caused alarm in the capital. Government claims that they were there simply to preserve order seemed to have been sincere – until the last week in June. On 26 June, 4,800 extra troops were ordered into the Paris region and on 1 July, 11,500 more. In less than a week the strength of army units called to Paris increased from under 4,000 to over 20,000. It was impossible to doubt any longer that the King and his advisers had decided to dissolve the National Assembly, by force if necessary. In this desperate situation the Assembly was saved by the revolt of the people of Paris.

6 The Economic Crisis

KEY ISSUE What impact did the economic crisis have on the outbreak of the revolution?

In the late 1770s a depression began which affected the whole economy, apart from the colonial trade. Wine prices collapsed because of overproduction. This was disastrous for many peasants, for whom wine was an important cash crop. Poor harvests happened more frequently – in 1778–9, 1781–2 and 1785–6.[6] In 1788 there was a major disaster. There was a very wet spring and freak hailstones in many areas in July resulting in a very poor harvest. A bad harvest in a pre-industrial society always led to massive unemployment, as the resulting rise in the price of food led to less demand for manufactured goods, at a time when both peasants and urban workers needed employment more than ever to cope with the higher prices. Textiles, which accounted for half of industrial production, were particularly badly hit. They were already affected by the Eden Treaty of 1786, which came into operation in May 1787 and allowed imports of English goods, including textiles, at reduced import duties. Production and employment in the textile industries fell by 50 per cent in 1789.

In normal times a worker spent up to 50 per cent of his income on bread. In August 1788 the price of a 1.8 kg loaf was 9 sous (1 Livre = 20 sous), by March 1789 it had risen to over 14 sous per loaf. By the spring of 1789 a Parisian worker could be spending 88 per cent of his wages on bread. On 28 April the house and factory of a prosperous wallpaper manufacturer, Réveillon, were set on fire, as it was rumoured that he was going to reduce wages. But this riot was more a violent protest against the scarcity and high price of bread than a protest against wages. At least 50 people were killed or wounded by troops. The situation was therefore very volatile when the Estates-General met. Economic issues (the price of bread and employment) were, for the first time, pushing France towards revolution, and had created discontent which could be used by political groups to bring crowds on to the streets to save the National Assembly. The economic crisis contributed to the emergence of a 'popular movement', of discontented workers and small traders.

7 The Revolt in Paris – the Storming of the Bastille

KEY ISSUE What was the significance of the storming of the Bastille?

In late June, journalists and politicians established a permanent headquarters in the Palais Royal in Paris, home of the Duc d'Orléans. Here thousands gathered each night to listen to revolutionary speakers. It was the Palais Royal that directed the popular movement.

By 11 June Louis had about 30,000 troops round Paris and Versailles and felt strong enough to dismiss Necker, who was at the height of his popularity and regarded as the people's chief supporter in the government. The deputies, alarmed, thought that Louis would dissolve the Assembly and arrest its leading members.

When news of Necker's dismissal reached Paris the next day, Parisians flocked to the Palais Royal, where speakers called on them to take up arms. A frantic search began for muskets and ammunition. On the same day crowds of poor Parisians attacked the hated customs posts, which surrounded Paris and imposed duties on goods, including food, entering the city. Out of 54 posts, 40 were destroyed. This action had not been planned but it frightened the respectable citizens of Paris, who feared that attacks on property and looting would follow. To gain control of the situation and prevent the indiscriminate arming of the population the Paris electors (representatives of the 60 electoral districts which had chosen the deputies to the Estates-General) set up a committee to act as a government of the city. They formed a National Guard or citizens' militia, from which most workers would be excluded. It had the double purpose of protecting property against the attacks of the *menu peuple* and of defending Paris against any possible attack by royal troops. It was these electors and the supporters of the Duc d'Orléans who were to turn what had begun as spontaneous riots into a general rising.

a) The Fall of the Bastille

Their search for weapons took Parisians to the Invalides, an old soldiers' retirement home which also served as an arsenal, where they seized over 28,000 muskets and 20 cannon. They were still short of gunpowder and cartridges, so they marched on the fortress of the Bastille. This imposing royal prison was a permanent reminder of the power of the *ancien régime*. The government could have used its troops to crush the rising but they were proving unreliable. By late June many French Guards, who worked at various trades in Paris in their off-duty hours and mixed with the population, were being influenced by agitators at the Palais Royal. Discipline in this élite unit

The Storming of the Bastille, 14 July 1789

deteriorated rapidly. As early as 24 June two companies had refused to go on duty. By 14 July, 5 out of 6 battalions of French Guards had deserted and some joined the Parisians besieging the Bastille. There were 5,000 other troops nearby, but the officers told their commander that they could not rely on their men. Troops were removed from the streets of Paris to the Champ de Mars, where they did nothing.

The crowd outside the Bastille were denied entry. The governor de Launay refused to hand over any gunpowder. There was no intention to storm the fortress, although a group managed to enter the inner courtyard. De Launay ordered his troops to open fire on them. Parisians were killed. French Guards supporting the crowd, using cannon taken from the Invalides that morning, overcame the defenders. De Launay was forced to surrender. He was murdered and decapitated by an enraged crowd. Those who had taken part in the attack on the Bastille were not wealthy middle class but *sans-culottes*. At the height of the rebellion about a quarter of a million Parisians were under arms. This was the first and most famous of the *journées*, which occurred at decisive moments during the course of the revolution.

The events in Paris on 14 July had far-reaching results. The King had lost control of Paris, where the electors set up a Commune to run the city and made Lafayette commander of the National Guard. The Assembly (which on 7 July had taken the name of the National Constituent Assembly) began to draw up a constitution safe from the threat of being dissolved by the King. Real power had passed from the King to the elected representatives of the people. Louis was no longer in a position to dictate to the Assembly, because he could not rely upon the army. J.M. Roberts believes that 14 July is a strong candidate for the day on which the French Revolution began. 'It was a great psychological and symbolic turning point, for it made apparent something that had been true since May: the old absolute monarchy of France was dead. Unless imposed by foreign arms, there could now be no reversal of the fact that the National Assembly shared power with the King.'[7] When news of the fall of the Bastille spread through France, the peasant revolution, which had already begun, was extended and intensified. The revolt of Paris also led to the emigration of some nobles, led by the King's brother the Comte d'Artois: 20,000 fled abroad in two months.

On 17 July the King journeyed to Paris, where the people gave him a hostile reception. Louis recognised the new revolutionary council – the Commune – and the National Guard, and wore in his hat the red, white and blue cockade of the Revolution (red and blue – the colours of Paris, were added to the white of the Bourbons). The significance of the King's humiliation was not lost on foreign diplomats. The British ambassador, the Duke of Dorset, wrote:

> the greatest Revolution that we know anything of has been effected with . . . the loss of very few lives: from this moment we may consider France as a free country; the King a limited monarch and the nobility as reduced to a level with the rest of the nation.

Gouverneur Morris, later the US ambassador to France, told George Washington: 'You may consider the revolution to be over, since the authority of the King and the nobles has been utterly destroyed'.

b) The Municipal Revolution

As a consequence of the revolt of Paris the authority of the King collapsed in most French towns. His orders would now be obeyed only if they had been approved by the Constituent Assembly. Citizens' militias were set up in several towns, such as Marseille, before the National Guard was formed in Paris, and in some other towns revolutionaries seized power before they did so in the capital. However, most provincial towns waited to hear what had happened in Paris before they acted and this could take up to a fortnight. 'The Parisian spirit of commotion', wrote Arthur Young from Strasbourg on 21 July, 'spreads quickly'. Nearly everywhere there was a municipal revolution in which the bourgeoisie played a leading part. This took various forms. In some towns the old council merely broadened its membership and carried on as before. In Bordeaux the electors of the Third Estate seized control, closely following the example of Paris. In most towns, including Lille, Rouen and Lyon, the old municipal corporations were overthrown by force. In nearly every town a National Guard was formed which, as in Paris, was designed both to control popular violence and prevent counter-revolution. Nearly all intendants abandoned their posts. The King had lost control of Paris and of the provincial towns. He was to lose control of the countryside through the peasant revolution.

8 The Peasant Revolution

> **KEY ISSUE** To what extent did the peasantry make gains during 1789?

a) The Rural Revolt and the Great Fear

The peasants played no part in the events which led up to revolution until the spring of 1789. It was the bad harvest of 1788 which gave them a role, because of the great misery and hardship in the countryside. Most peasants had to buy their bread and were, therefore, badly affected by the rise in the price of bread in the spring and summer of 1789. Many also suffered from the unemployment in the textile industry, as they wove cloth in order to survive. From January 1789 grain convoys and the premises of suspected hoarders were attacked. This was normal in times of dearth and would probably have died out when the new crop was harvested in the summer.

What made these food riots more important than usual were the political events which were taking place. The calling of the Estates-General aroused general excitement amongst the peasants. They believed that the King would not have asked them to state their grievances in the *cahiers* if he did not intend to do something about them. The lieutenant-general of the Saumur district commented:

1 What is really tiresome is that these [electoral] assemblies . . . have generally believed themselves invested with some sovereign authority and that when they came to an end, the peasants went home with the idea that henceforward they were free from tithes, hunting prohibitions and
5 the payment of seigneurial dues.

The fall of the Bastille also had a tremendous effect in the countryside. Risings immediately followed in Normandy and Franche Comté. Demonstrations and riots against taxes, the tithe and feudal dues spread throughout the country, so that it appeared that law and order had collapsed everywhere.

On the great estates of the Church and other landowners were storehouses of grain, which had been collected as rents, feudal dues and tithes. In the spring and summer of 1789 they were the only places where grain was held in bulk. Landlords were regarded as hoarders and their châteaux were attacked. They were also attacked because that is where the *terriers* listing peasant obligations were kept. On 28 June the President of the Grenoble parlement wrote:

1 There is daily talk of attacking the nobility, of setting fire to their
   châteaux in order to burn all their title-deeds . . . In cantons where
   unrest has been less sensational, the inhabitants meet daily to pass resolutions that they will pay no more rent or other seigneurial dues but
5 fix a moderate price for their redemption and lower the rate of the
   lods; endless hostile projects spring from that spirit of equality and independence which prevails on men's minds today.

Hundreds of châteaux were ransacked and many were set on fire but
there was remarkably little bloodshed – landowners or their agents
were killed only when they resisted.

The attack on the châteaux was caught up in what became known
as the Great Fear, which lasted from 20 July to 6 August 1789. It began
in local rumours that bands of brigands, in the pay of the aristocracy,
were going to destroy the harvest. The peasants took up arms to await
the brigands and when they did not appear, turned their anger
against the landlords. The Great Fear spread the peasant rising
throughout most of France. Some areas on the periphery, such as
Brittany, Alsace and the Basque region, were unaffected.

b) The August Decrees

The Assembly was in a dilemma. It could not ask the King's troops to
crush the peasants, because afterwards they might be turned against
the Assembly itself. Yet they could not allow the anarchy in the countryside to continue. This could be ended and the support of the peasants gained for the Assembly and for the Revolution, by giving them
at least part of what they wanted. On 3 August leaders of the 'patriot'
party drew up a plan for liberal nobles to propose the dismantling of
the feudal system. On the night of 4 August the Vicomte de Noailles,
followed by the Duc d'Auguillon, one of the richest landowners in
France, proposed that obligations concerned with personal servitude
should be abolished without compensation: these included serfdom
and the *corvée*. Other rights such as *champart* and *lods et ventes* were
regarded as a form of property and were to be redeemed (paid for by
the peasant). But these were the dues which affected the peasant most
severely, so there was little satisfaction in the countryside with the
limited nature of the reforms. These proposals were given legal form
in the decrees of 5–11 August, which began:

1 The National Assembly abolishes the feudal system entirely. It decrees
   that, as regards feudal rights and dues . . . those relating . . . to personal
   serfdom . . . are abolished without compensation; all the others are
   declared to be redeemable and the rate and mode of redemption will
5 be determined by the National Assembly. Those of the aforementioned
   rights which are not abolished by this decree will continue to be collected until their owners have been compensated.
   All seigneurial courts are abolished without any compensation.

Amid great excitement, the example of Noailles and Auguillon was followed by other noble deputies, who queued up to renounce their privileges in a spirit of patriotic fervour. The changes proposed went far beyond what had been proposed in the *cahiers*.

1   All forms of tithe . . . are abolished, subject to making alternative provision for the expenses of divine worship, payment of priests, poor relief etc. . . . to which they are at present allocated. Venality of judicial and municipal offices is abolished with immediate effect. Justice will be
5   administered without charge. Financial privileges, whether relating to persons or to land, in matters of taxation are abolished for all time. Payment will fall on all citizens and all lands, in the same manner . . .
       Since a national constitution and public liberty are more advantageous to the provinces than the privileges which some of them enjoy
10 and which must be scarified for the sake of the intimate union of all the parts of the empire, it is declared that all the special privileges of the provinces, principalities, pays, cantons, towns and village communes, are abolished forever and assimilated into the common rights of all Frenchmen.
15   All citizens, without distinction of birth, are eligible for all offices and dignities, whether ecclesiastical, civil or military.

When the Assembly adjourned at 2 am on 5 August the deputies were weeping for joy. One of the deputies Duquesnoy exclaimed 'What a nation! What glory. What honour to the French!'. Bailly, the Mayor of Paris, in his account of the session, stressed the revolutionary nature of the decrees:

1   Never before have so many bodies and individuals voted such sacrifices at one time, in such generous terms and with such unanimity. This has been a night for destruction and for public happiness. We may view this moment as the dawn of a new revolution, when all the burdens weigh-
5   ing on the people were abolished and France was truly reborn. The feudal regime which had oppressed the people for centuries was demolished at a stroke and in an instant. The National Assembly achieved more for the people in a few hours than the wisest and most enlightened nations had done for many centuries.

Some writers did not share Bailly's views regarding the reforms. The journalist Marat was less than enthusiastic. In his paper *L'Ami du people* (21 September 1789) Marat told his readers that:

1   'The National Assembly has passed a number of decrees which have been praised to the skies. If these sacrifices were dictated by benevolence, then we must agree that they waited a long while before it raised its voice. It is by the light of the flames of their burning chateaux that
5   they have found the greatness of spirit to renounce the privilege of keeping in fetters (chains) men who have already recovered their liberty by force'.

How important were the August Decrees? They marked the end of noble power and the privilege of birth by establishing a society based on civil equality. All Frenchmen had the same rights and duties, could enter any profession according to their ability and would pay the same taxes. Of course, equality in theory was different from equality in practice. The career open to talent benefited the bourgeoisie rather than the peasant or worker, as they lacked the education to take advantage of it. Nevertheless, French society would never be the same again – the old society of orders had gone.

The peasants – the vast mass of the population – were committed to the new regime, at least in so far as it removed their feudal obligations. They did not like having to compensate landowners for the loss of their feudal dues. Many stopped paying them, until they were finally abolished without compensation in 1793. Some, in areas such as Brittany and the Vendée, were to become active opponents of the Revolution (see Chapter 4), but for most of them the Revolution marked the end of the feudal system and they feared that if they did not support it, aristocratic privilege and the tithe would return and they would lose all they had gained.

The August Decrees had swept away institutions like the provincial estates and cleared the way for a national, uniform system of administration. As most institutions had been based on privilege, the Assembly now began the laborious task, which would take two years to complete, of changing those concerned with local government, law, finance, the Church (whose income was halved by the loss of the tithe, so that it could no longer carry the burden of funding education, hospitals and poor relief), and the armed forces. Yet many thought that those who had lost power would try to recover it. There was a widespread fear of an aristocratic plot and a feeling that, without constant vigilance, the victories of July and August could be quickly reversed. As Châteaubriand noted, 'The patricians (nobles) began the revolution, the plebeians (ordinary citizen) finished it'.[8]

References

1   Georges Lefebvre, *The Coming of the French Revolution* (Vintage Books, 1947), p. 5.
2   Albert Soboul, *The French Revolution 1787–1799. From the Storming of the Bastille to Napoleon* (Unwin/Hymen, 1989), p. 98.
3   William Doyle, *The Oxford History of the French Revolution* (Oxford, 1989), p. 68.
4   Florin Aftalion, *The French Revolution. An Economic Interpretation*, (Cambridge, 1990) p. 24.
5   Alexis de Tocqueville, *The Ancien Régime and the French Revolution*, (1856, English language edition Collins, 1966) Pt 3, Chs 3 and 4.
6   Colin Jones, *The Longman Companion to the French Revolution*, (Longman, 1990) p. 284.
7   J.M. Roberts, *The French Revolution*, (Oxford Univ Press, 1978) p. 18.
8   Châteaubriand, François René, Viscount de (1768–1848), a celebrated author who fought with the *émigré* army.

Summary Diagram
The Origins of the French Revolution

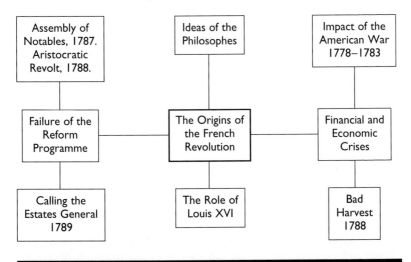

Assembly of Notables, 1787. Aristocratic Revolt, 1788.	Ideas of the Philosophes	Impact of the American War 1778–1783
Failure of the Reform Programme	The Origins of the French Revolution	Financial and Economic Crises
Calling the Estates General 1789	The Role of Louis XVI	Bad Harvest 1788

Working on Chapter 2

This is a key chapter in the book. It sets out and covers a great deal of ground relating to the origin of the Revolution. Many political crises have their origins in severe economic problems. It is very important that you try and understand how economic and financial difficulties led to demands for reform. Study carefully who started the reform movement and why it failed. You should also note the role of Paris in the emerging crisis and how and why the revolution spread to the rest of France. Your notes should help you to understand why there was a revolution in France in 1789. At each stage of the argument you should ask yourself three questions: Why did an event occur? What is its significance? How does it link up with other events?

Answering structured and essay questions on Chapter 2

Many of the questions on the topic covered in this chapter will revolve around how or why the French revolution started. Structured questions will usually consist of two parts with the first being easier than the second. Consider the following examples:

I **a)** Outline briefly the main features of the financial crisis 1786–8. (*8 marks*)
   b) To what extent did the financial crisis contribute to the demands for reform? (*12 marks*)

2 a) Explain briefly how the peasants stood to gain from the measures agreed on 4th August 1789. (*8 marks*)
  b) Is it accurate that Paris was dominating the course of the revolution in 1789? Explain your answer fully. (*12 marks*)

Examiners will award low marks to essays which use a narrative approach, and/or do not answer the question directly. They are looking for an ability to construct a relevant argument which addresses the issue(s) posed in an analytical manner. Questions will expect you to evaluate. They may open with 'Why' or the phrases 'To what extent'. They may take the form of a quotation, which you are asked to discuss. The quotation will usually be selected to provide you with an opportunity to construct an argument, which may well challenge the view expressed, although it is totally acceptable to agree with the quotation if you think the interpretation it contains is correct. Questions on the causes of the Revolution tend to fall into three groups:

1 The social groups or classes which wanted a revolution.
2 The political, economic or financial origins of the Revolution.
3 The role of the monarchy in bringing about revolution.

Typical questions are:

1 'Was the French Revolution a revolution of all classes of society against the old system of government?'

Write down the names of the classes. Then divide each class into different groups (e.g. divide nobles into courtiers, noblesse de robe and provincial nobility). Did all the groups have the same interests? Make lists of those who supported and those who opposed the 'old system of government'. Why did they do so?

2 To what extent was the storming of the Bastille on the 14th July the most significant event during 1789?

The key phrase in the question is 'most significant'. You are asked to evaluate the extent to which the most dramatic event of the year was also the most significant. Set out ways in which it merits this description – the symbolism of the fall etc. You will also need to balance the answer by challenging the notion and providing possible alternatives – the Tennis Court oath, the Night of the 4th of August. The structure of this and most other essays should be: i) Introduction – relate to the question and suggest a line of response, ii) the main body of the essay, containing several paragraphs where you consider arguments for and arguments against the view expressed in the quotation. Try and aim for a balanced and considered response, and iii) a Conclusion which draws together in summary form the main arguments in your essay.

3 'Was it the absolute power of the French monarchy or its weakness that caused the Revolution of 1789?'

For the 'absolute power of the French monarchy' you will have to refer to your notes from Chapter 1. In what sense was the French monarchy absolute? You may decide that it was not absolute and that it was the limitations on its power (e.g. the privileges of the *parlements*) that enabled opposition to make itself heard and to grow. In what sense was the monarchy 'weak' – structurally or because Louis XVI was a feeble king? What did he do which showed he was weak? Did his actions lead to revolution? Provide examples of his actions.

Answering source-based questions on Chapter 2

1. The Cahiers
Read the *cahier* on page 23 and then answer the following questions:

a) Explain briefly the reference to 'shakled and confined by the bonds of feudalism'. (line 1) (*2 marks*)
b) What information may be inferred from the source about the demands of the peasantry in 1789? (*8 marks*)
c) How useful is the source to an understanding of conditions in the French countryside before 1789? (*20 marks*)

2. The August Decrees
Read carefully the selection from the August Decrees on pages 31–2 and Bailly's and Marat's views on page 32, then answer the following questions:

a) Explain the reference to 'Venality of judicial and municipal offices is abolished'. (page 32, lines 3–4). (*4 marks*)
b) How reliable is Bailly's account of the events? (*4 marks*)
c) Compare the views of Bailly and Marat. In what way do they differ in their evaluation of the events which had taken place? (*8 marks*)
d) Using the sources and your background knowledge, did the August decrees satisfy peasant demands? (*14 marks*)

3 The Revolution and the Monarchy, 1789–92

POINTS TO CONSIDER

This chapter considers two very important issues:1) the nature of the reform programmes which were undertaken by the National and Legislative Assemblies, and the extent to which they changed France, and 2) why the monarchy was overthrown and replaced by a republic. During your first reading of the chapter, note very carefully the nature and significance of the reforms. You will also need to consider the causes of the emergence of a republican movement, and the extent to which Louis was responsible for the eventual overthrow of the monarchy.

KEY DATES

1789 26 Aug Declaration of the Rights of Man and the Citizen
5–6 Oct 'October days'. Louis XVI and the National Assembly moved to Paris
2 Nov Church property nationalised
1790 12 July Civil Constitution of the Clergy
Aug Reform of the legal system and the abolition of the *parlements*
1791 20 June Flight to Varennes
17 July Champ de Mars massacre
14 Sept Louis XVI accepted the new constitution
1792 20 April War declared on Austria
10 Aug Overthrow of the Monarchy

1 The Revolution Consolidated

> **KEY ISSUES** What was the significance of the Declaration of the Rights of Man and the Citizen? How important were the October days?

The August Decrees prepared the ground for the creation of a constitution. Before this, the deputies drew up the principles on which this should be based – the Declaration of the Rights of Man and the Citizen (August 1789). It condemned the practices of the *ancien régime* and outlined the rights of citizens, as demanded in the *cahiers* of all three orders. The following are selected extracts from the Declaration:

The Declaration of the Rights of Man and the Citizen, 1789

1 Men are born free and equal in their rights.
2 The aim of every political association is the maintenance of the natural and imprescriptible rights of man. Those rights are those of liberty, property, security and resistance to oppression.
3 The fundamental source of all sovereignty resides in the nation.
4 Liberty consists in being able to do anything which does not harm another.
7 No man may be accused, arrested or detained except in cases determined by the law.
10 No one must be troubled on account of his opinions, even his religious beliefs, provided that their expression does not disturb public order under the law.
11 Free expression of thought and opinions is one of the most precious rights of man. Accordingly, every citizen may speak, write and publish freely.
13 General taxation is indispensable for the upkeep of the public force and for the expenses of government. It should be borne equally by all the citizens in proportion to their means.
14 Every citizen has the right, in person or through his representative, to establish the necessity for a tax, freely to consent to it.
17 . . . the right to property is inviolable and sacred.

The Declaration was to long outlast the constitution to which it was later attached and was to be an inspiration to liberals throughout Europe in the nineteenth century (see page 138). For all its well meaning sentiments, the Declaration mainly represented the interests of the property owning bourgeoisie. Its significance is that '. . . it sounded the death-knell of the Ancien Régime, while preparing the public for the constructive legislation that was to follow'.[1]

The King did not share the general enthusiasm for the changes that were taking place and on 5 August he wrote to the Archbishop of Arles: 'I will never consent to the spoliation of my clergy and of my nobility. I will not sanction decrees by which they are despoiled'. He could not use force against the Assembly as the loyalty of the army was in doubt, with many offices and men sympathetic to the revolution. Louis adopted instead a policy of non-cooperation and refused to officially support the August Decrees and the Declaration of Rights.

This forced the Assembly to consider the important question of what rights the King should have. Should he be able to veto or delay legislation passed by the Assembly? The deputies decided that the King should have a 'suspensive veto' – the power to suspend or delay all laws other than financial ones passed by the Assembly for a period up to four years.

No-one, at this stage considered abolishing the monarchy and setting up a republic. It was decided that legislative power should reside with the National Assembly and that no taxes or loans could be raised without its consent, while '. . . supreme executive power resides exclusively in the King's hands'.

The King refused to approve the Assembly's decrees, but was forced to do so by another revolutionary *journée*. This was prompted by a banquet, held by the King's Guards at Versailles on 1 October to celebrate the arrival of the Flanders regiment, during which there were anti-revolutionary demonstrations. Officers trampled on the tricolour cockade and replaced it with the white cockade of the Bourbons. When news of this reached Paris feelings ran high and there were demands that the King should be brought back to the capital.

This demand coincided with a food shortage in Paris. On 5 October a crowd of women stormed the *Hôtel de Ville*, the headquarters of the Commune, demanding bread. They were persuaded to march to Versailles to put their complaints to the King and the Assembly. Six or seven thousand of them set off on the five-hour march. Later in the day 20,000 National Guards, under Lafayette, followed them. When the women reached Versailles they invaded the Assembly and sent a deputation to the King, who agreed to provide Paris with grain. He also agreed to approve the August Decrees and the Declaration of Rights. On 6 October at the request of the crowd, the King and Queen appeared on a balcony and were greeted with cries of 'To Paris'. That afternoon the royal family left Versailles.

The 'October Days' was a very significant event in the early phase of the Revolution. Once in Paris the King regarded himself as a prisoner of the Paris mob and therefore not bound by anything he was forced to accept. When Parisians had revolted in July they had seen the Assembly as their ally. In October the Assembly had been ignored and humiliated. When the deputies followed the King to Paris, some of them felt as much imprisoned as the King did. Most deputies wanted to work out a compromise with Louis, but this was much more difficult for them in Paris, surrounded by a population which could impose its will on the Assembly by another *journée*. Following the 'October Days' the Assembly issued a decree which changed the title and status of the monarch, from 'King of France and Navarre' to 'Louis, by the grace of God and the constitutional law of the State, King of the French'. Louis was now subordinate to the law, and his subjects now became citizens. There had been a shift in the balance of power towards Paris and its increasingly politicized population. Mercy Argentau, the Austrian ambassador, realised this soon after the fall of the Bastille, when he wrote:

1 However unbelievable the Revolution that has just been accomplished may appear, it is none the less absolutely certain that from now on the city of Paris has assumed the role of a king in France and that it can, if it pleases, send an army of forty to fifty thousand citizens to surround
5 the Assembly and dictate laws to it.

From now on the moderate majority of deputies distrusted the population of Paris as much as they did the King, although it was the popular *journées* which had enabled them to defeat Louis in the first place.

2 The Reforms of the Constituent Assembly

> **KEY ISSUE** In what ways did the Constituent Assembly reform the French state?

After October 1789 most Frenchmen believed that the Revolution was over. For the next year there was broad agreement amongst the different groups in the Assembly, as they set about reorganising French government, laws, finances and the economy. In doing this they tried to apply the principles of the Declaration of Rights and give France a uniform, decentralised, representative and humanitarian system. The deputies regarded themselves as heirs of the Enlightenment and sought to end conflict, cruelty, superstition and poverty. Though nearly everyone wanted to retain a limited monarchy, there were few regrets about the passing of the *ancien régime*. France was fundamentally changed in many ways. New institutions and attitudes took root that have survived until the present day.

a) Local Government

In restructuring local government the deputies wanted to make sure that power was decentralised, passing from the central government in Paris to the local authorities. This would make it much more difficult for the King to recover the power he had held before the Revolution. It was hoped that the administrative chaos of the *ancien régime* would be replaced by a coherent and rational structure. The Assembly also wanted to ensure that all officials would be elected and would be responsible to those who elected them.

By decrees of December 1789 and January 1790 France was divided into 83 departments, which were subdivided into 547 districts and 43,360 communes (or municipalities). Communes were grouped into cantons, where primary assemblies for elections were held and justices of the peace had their courts. All these administrative divisions, except the cantons, were run by elected councils.

The reforms which revealed the real intention of the Assembly related to voting qualifications. It became clear that deputies did not intend that those who had taken part in the popular protests should have a direct role in government. A decree in October 1789 introduced the concept of 'active citizens', of which there were in essence three tiers. The first consisted of men over 25 who paid the equivalent of three days' labour in taxes. It was estimated in 1790 that almost 4.3 million Frenchmen fell into this category. Citizens who did not pay this amount in taxes had no vote and were known as 'passive' citizens. In reality the only thing active citizens could do was to choose electors – the second tier. An elector had to be an active citizen who paid the equivilent of ten days labour in local taxes. About 50,000 men met this qualification. This second tier of 'active' citizens elected members of the district and department assemblies and could become officials there. They also elected the deputies to the National Assembly. To be eligible to become a deputy in the National Assembly – the third tier – an 'active citizen' had to pay at least a *marc d' argent* (a silver mark), the equivalent to 54 days' manual labour, in direct taxation.

The electoral system was, therefore, heavily weighted in favour of the wealthy, although 61 per cent of Frenchmen had the right to take part in some elections (in England only 4 per cent of adult males had the vote). At local level most peasants had the right to vote and were qualified to stand for office. This amounted to an administrative revolution. Before 1789 government officials ran the provincial administration: there was not one elected council. In 1790 there were no government officials at the local level: elected councils had totally replaced them.

Who controlled these councils? In the south, bourgeois landowners controlled them. In the north, the bourgeoisie was largely urban and took office in the towns, which left the rural communes in the hands of *laboureurs*, small merchants and artisans. People belonging to social groups which had never held any public office now had the opportunity of doing so. It is estimated that in the decade 1789–99 about a million people were elected to councils and gained experience in local administration. These councils had an enormous burden of work thrust upon them in December 1789 – much more than the *cahiers* had asked for. They had to assess and collect direct taxes, maintain law and order, carry out public works, see to the upkeep of churches and control the National Guard. Later legislation added to their responsibilities: they had to administer the clerical oath of loyalty; register births, marriages and deaths; requisition grain; and keep a watch on people suspected of opposing the Revolution.

How effective were the councils in carrying out their many duties? In the towns there was usually an adequate supply of literate, talented people, who provided a competent administration. In the villages it was often impossible to fill the councils with men who could read and write. Rural communes, therefore, often carried out their duties badly. In strongly Catholic areas officials disliked persecuting priests who had refused to take the oath of loyalty. Consequently, many resigned and areas were left without any effective local government.

b) Finance

After the royal administration collapsed in 1789 few taxes were collected. The Assembly needed money quickly, particularly when it decided that venal office-holders should be compensated for the loss of their offices. Yet a new tax system could not be set up immediately. It decided, therefore, that the existing system of direct and indirect taxation should continue until 1791. This was very unpopular. People wanted the demands made in the *cahiers* to be met at once. When there were outbreaks of violence in Picardy, one of the most heavily taxed areas under the *ancien régime*, the government gave way. The gabelle was abolished in March 1790 and within a year nearly all the unpopular indirect taxes, except for external customs duties, were also abolished.

To provide money for the state in the period before the new system operated effectively, the Assembly voted in November 1789 that church property was 'at the disposal of the nation'. Church lands would be sold for the benefit of the state, which would then be responsible for paying the clergy because the Church would have lost most of its income (it had already lost the tithe). The sale was seen as guaranteeing the success of the Revolution: those who bought church lands would have a vested interest in maintaining it, as a restoration of the *ancien régime* might lead to the Church recovering its land. It was also hoped that the clergy would support the new regime, as they would be dependent on it for their salaries. The government would issue bonds, soon known as *assignats*, which the public would buy and use for the purchase of church lands. In April 1790 the Assembly converted the bonds into paper money, like bank notes, which could be used in all financial transactions.

Who bought the church lands or *biens nationaux* ('national properties'), as they were known? Sales of land in 1791–2 were brisk. For example, in Haute-Marne nearly 39,000 hectares of church land representing a tenth of the arable land in the department was sold.[2] The main beneficiaries were the bourgeoisie, as they had significant amounts of ready cash available. This was necessary because the *biens* were sold off in large plots. Members of the bourgeoisie bought most of the available land near the towns. Peasants fared better away from the towns. Lefebvre made a special study of the Nord department and found that by 1799 25 per cent of the land there had been sold as *biens nationaux*: of this peasants had bought 52 per cent and the bourgeoisie 48 per cent.[3] About a third of the peasants were first-time owners, so land did not go only to the wealthier *laboureurs*. Even where the bourgeoisie bought most of the land, they often resold it piecemeal to the peasants, especially in the east. It is estimated that the number of peasant smallholders increased by a million between 1789 and 1810.

The new financial system began in January 1791. As indirect taxes were abolished, the main tax was one on land, to replace the *taille* and the *vingtième*. This was like the tax proposed by Calonne in 1787 and was expected to bring in 75 per cent of total receipts. Twenty per cent was to come from a property tax, which people complained was the old capitation in a new form, and the rest from customs duties. Municipal councils were to collect the taxes. This system might have worked well if there had been a systematic valuation of the land, but for this a large number of officials was needed. The Assembly would not provide them, as they would cost too much. Consequently, a survey of land values was not begun until 1807 and was not completed until the 1830s. Meanwhile, the new tax rolls were based on those of the *ancien régime*, so that great regional variations remained. People in the Seine et Marne department, for example, paid five times as much in taxes as those in the Arriège.

Was the new system better than the old? The poor certainly benefited, as the burden of taxation fell on producers rather than consumers, with the abolition of indirect taxes. It was a fairer system, as all property and income was to be taxed on the same basis. There would no longer be any special privileges or exemptions. Citizens would pay according to their means. The new financial structure was to last in its essentials throughout the nineteenth century.

c) Economic Reforms

All the deputies in the Constituent Assembly believed in *laissez-faire*: that trade and industry should be free from any government interference. Therefore, they introduced free trade in grain in August 1789 and removed price controls. These measures were extended to other products in 1790–91, though this is not what the people as a whole desired. They wanted the price and distribution of all essential goods to be controlled, in order to avoid scarcity, high prices and possible starvation. In October 1790 internal tariffs were abolished, so a national market was created for the first time. This was helped by the creation of a single system of weights and measures – the decimal system – which applied to the whole of France.

The deputies were determined to get rid of any corporations which had special privileges. Guilds were therefore abolished in 1791, as they restricted the entry of people into certain trades. In June 1791 a coalition of 80,000 Parisian workers was threatening a general strike to obtain higher wages, so the Assembly passed the Le Chapelier law, named after the deputy who proposed it, which forbade trade unions and employers' organisations. Collective bargaining, picketing and strikes were declared illegal. 'One of the master strokes of capitalism and the spirit of free enterprise'.[4] No one in the Assembly objected. Strikes remained illegal until 1864. The ban on trade unions was not lifted until 1884.

The Assembly regarded relief for the poor as a duty of the state. The Church had provided what little assistance the poor had received but it could do so no longer when it lost its main sources of income. Therefore, there was an urgent need for a national organisation, financed by taxation, to take over this role. The Assembly set up a committee which, in 1791, showed for the first time just how serious the problem was. It concluded that nearly two million people could support themselves only by begging. When it came to taking practical measures to help the poor, the committee found itself impotent. There was simply not enough money available to deal with such an appalling problem, so nothing was done.

d) Justice

The Constituent Assembly applied the same principle of uniformity to the legal system as it had done to local government. Instead of different systems of law in the north and south and different types of law court, there were to be the same law and law-courts throughout France. *Lettres de cachet* had already been made illegal by the Declaration of Rights. Between 1789 and 1792 all the old law courts – the *parlements*, seigneurial and ecclesiastical courts – were swept away and replaced by a new, uniform system, which was based on the administrative divisions of the reformed local government. In each canton there was to be a justice of the peace, who handled many cases which had previously gone to the seigneurial courts. His main task was to persuade the different parties to come to an agreement but he could also judge minor civil cases without appeal. More serious civil cases went to the district court. There was to be a criminal court in each department, where trials would be held in public and a jury of 12 citizens, chosen by ballot, would decide on questions of guilt or innocence. The idea of having a jury, like that of having justices of the peace, was taken from English law. At the head of the judicial system was a Court of Appeal, whose judges were elected by the department assemblies. All judges were elected by active citizens but only those who had been lawyers for five years could be elected. This ensured that all judges were well qualified and accountable.

There were other changes which also improved the quality of French justice. The penal code was made more humane: torture and mutilation were abolished. Anyone arrested had to be brought before a court within 24 hours. The number of crimes for which death was the penalty was vastly reduced. In March 1792 a new and more efficient method of execution – the guillotine was introduced. It replaced all other forms used on those condemned to death. This mechanical device with its angular blade would become one of the most feared and lasting images of the revolution. The new judicial system was one of the most lasting reforms of the Constituent Assembly. For the first time, justice was made free and equal to all, and was therefore popular. The French system of justice had been one of the most backward, barbarous and corrupt in Europe. In two years it became one of the most enlightened.

e) Religion

The Constituent Assembly wanted to create a church that was free from abuses, free from foreign (papal) control, democratic, and linked to the new system of local government. The deputies were not in the main anti-religious or anti-Catholic. They simply wanted to extend to religion the principles they applied elsewhere. They also wanted to tie the Catholic Church in France more closely to the state than it had been under the *ancien régime*, as this would strengthen the Revolution. They certainly had no intention of interfering with the doctrines of the Church or with its spiritual functions.

In August 1789 the Assembly abolished the tithe, annates (payments made by the French Church to the Pope) and pluralism (any person holding more than one clerical office, such as a bishopric). It also ended the privileges of the Church, such as its right to decide how much taxation it would pay. Most parish clergy supported these measures. They also accepted the sale of church lands, because they would be paid more than they had been under the *ancien régime*. In February 1790 a decree distinguished between monastic orders which did not work in the community and those which provided education and charity. The former were suppressed, as they made no direct contribution to the common good. The latter were allowed to remain 'for the present', although the taking of religious vows was forbidden. These changes took place without creating much of a stir among the clergy as a whole. Less popular was the decree in December 1789 giving civil rights to Protestants. These rights were extended to Jews in September 1791.

There was no serious conflict with the church until the Civil Constitution of the Clergy in July 1790. This adapted the organisation of the Church to the administrative framework of local government. Dioceses were to coincide with departments. This meant that the number of bishoprics would be reduced from 135 to 83. There would not only be fewer bishops but fewer clergy generally, as all clerical posts except for parish priests and bishops ceased to exist. The attempt to extend democracy to all aspects of government was also applied to the Church. But there was no intention of ending the Catholic Church's position as the State Church in France.

Most clergy opposed the principle of election but, even so, the majority (including many bishops) were in favour of finding a way of accepting the Civil Constitution. They demanded that the reforms be submitted to a national synod (assembly) of the French Church. This would have made a compromise possible but the Constituent Assembly would not agree to this, as it believed that it would have given the Church a privileged position in the state once again and a separate order, something which had just been abolished. As a church assembly was not allowed to discuss the matter, the clergy waited for the Pope to give his verdict. He delayed coming to a decision, as he was involved in delicate negotiations with the French

Extracts from the 'Civil Constitution of the Clergy', 12 July 1790.

Article. Title I. Concerning Ecclesiastical offices

1 Each department shall constitute a single diocese, and each diocese shall have the same extent and limits as the department.
4 No French church or parish and no French citizen may recognise, under any circumstance or on any pretext whatever, the authority of an ordinary or metropolitan bishop whose see is established under the control of a foreign power, nor of his delegates, whether residing in France or elsewhere.
20 All titles and offices, other than those mentioned in the present Constitution, are, from the day of publication of the present decree, abolished and suppressed, and their like may never be established.

Title II. Concerning Appointments to Ecclesiastical Benefices (positions)

1 From the day of publication of the present decree, election shall be the only means of appointment to bishoprics and livings.
2 All elections shall be by ballot and by absolute majority of votes.

Title III. Concerning Stipends (payment) of Ministers of Religion

1 Ministers of religion, performing the chief and most important duties of society shall be supported by the nation.

Title IV

1 The law of residence shall be observed rigorously (on all) without exception or distinction.
2 No bishop may be absent from his diocese for more than fifteen days consecutively in any year.

over the status of Avignon, papal territory inside France. The Assembly grew tired of waiting and in November 1790 decreed that clergy must take an oath to the Constitution. This split the clergy. In the Assembly only two of the 44 bishops and a third of the other clergy took the oath. In France as a whole seven bishops and 55 per cent of the clergy took the oath. When the Pope finally condemned the Civil Constitution in March and April 1791, many clergy who had taken the oath retracted.

The Civil Constitution of the Clergy had momentous results. It was one of the defining moments of revolution. It effectively destroyed the revolutionary consensus which had existed since 1789. Deputies in the Assembly were shocked when it was rejected by so many clergy and by the Pope. There were now in effect two Catholic Churches in France. One, the constitutional Church, accepted the Revolution and was rejected by Rome. The other, a non-juring Church (those who refused to take the oath were known as 'non-jurors' or 'refractories'), was approved the Pope but regarded by patriots as against the Revolution. 'Faced with what was crudely reduced to a stark choice between religion and revolution, half the adult population (and the great majority of women) rejected revolution'.[5] A major effect of this split was that the counter-revolution, the movement which sought to overturn the Revolution, received mass support for the first time. Before this, it had been supported only by a few royalists and *émigrés*. In the most strongly Catholic areas – the west, north-east and south of the Massif Central – few clergy took the oath. Many villagers complained that the Assembly was trying to change their religion, especially when refractory priests were expelled. They felt a sense of betrayal which, combined with their hostility to other measures of the Assembly, such as conscription, was to lead to open revolt in 1793 in areas such as the Vendée. Disaffection with the Revolution, which eventually turned into civil war, was, therefore, one result of the Civil Constitution of the Clergy. Another result was the King's attempt to flee from France in June 1791, precipitating a series of events which was to bring about the downfall of the monarchy.

f) The Constitution of 1791

One of the main aims of the Constituent Assembly had been to draw up a constitution, which would replace an absolute monarchy by a limited one. Real power was to pass to an elected assembly. Much of the Constitution – that the King should have a suspensive veto and that there should be one elected assembly – had been worked out in 1789 but the rest was not finally passed until September 1791. The King had the right to appoint his ministers (although they could not be members of the Assembly) and military commanders. His suspensive veto could not be applied to financial or constitutional matters. He was dependent on the Assembly for his foreign policy, as he needed its consent before he could declare war. The King, whose office was hereditary, was subordinate to the Assembly, as it passed the laws which the King had to obey. 'In France there is no authority superior to the law . . . it is only by means of the law that the King reigns'. In September the King was forced, reluctantly, to accept the Constitution. Marie Antoinette's attitude was that it was 'so monstrous that it cannot survive for long'. She was determined to overthrow it at the first opportunity.

3 The Revolutionary Clubs and Popular Discontent

> **KEY ISSUE** What was the impact of revolutionary clubs and the popular movement on the course of the French Revolution?

In the absence of political parties, clubs were established to support the protest movement. For large numbers of Frenchmen who had never experienced involvement in political life they provided a crash course in political education. Political clubs had begun to form soon after the Estates-General met in May 1789. The Jacobin Club originated in meetings of radical Breton deputies with others of similar views. When the Assembly moved to Paris after the October Days it met in premises rented from the Dominicans, who were nicknamed Jacobins. There its members debated measures that were to come before the Assembly. As it had a high entrance fee, its members – there were 1,200 by July 1790 – came mainly from the wealthiest sections of society. The dominant members of the Jacobin Club up to the summer of 1791 were liberal constitutional monarchists. Robespierre was the leader of a minority group of radical Jacobin deputies. A national network of Jacobin clubs soon grew up. By the end of 1793 there were over 2,000 Jacobin clubs. The greatest concentration was in the south-east. 'The Jacobin clubs were the principal instruments of political acculturation that some hundred thousand Frenchmen received between 1790 and 1799.'[6]

The Cordeliers Club, founded in April 1790, was more radical than the Jacobin Club and had unrestricted admission. It objected to the distinction between 'active' and 'passive' citizens and supported measures which the *sans-culottes* favoured: direct democracy, the recall of deputies to account for their actions, and the right of insurrection. It had much support among the working class, although its leaders were bourgeois. Danton and Desmoulins were lawyers. Hébert was an unsuccessful writer who had become a journalist when freedom of the press was allowed. Brissot was also a journalist. But the most notorious writer of all was Marat, a failed doctor. He hated all those who had enjoyed privileges under the old regime and attacked them violently in his newspaper, *L'Ami du Peuple*. He became the chief spokesman of the popular movement.

During the winter of 1790–91 the example of the Cordeliers Club led to the formation of many 'popular' or 'fraternal' societies, which were soon to be found in every district in Paris and in several provincial towns. In 1791 the Cordeliers Club and the popular societies formed a federation and elected a central committee. The members of the popular societies were drawn mainly from the liberal professions, officials, skilled artisans and shopkeepers. Labourers rarely joined, as they did not have the spare time for politics.

As there were no political parties, the clubs played an important part in the Revolution. They kept the public informed of the major issues of the day, supported election candidates and acted as pressure groups to influence deputies in the Assembly and to promote actions which the deputies seemed reluctant to undertake. In essence they provided education in political participation.

Peasants became dissatisfied with Revolution. When they realised in the spring of 1790 that their feudal dues were not abolished outright but would have to be bought out, they were deeply disillusioned. A rural revolution began in 1790 in Brittany, in central France and in the south-east. This lasted until 1792. Peasants fixed the price of grain, called for the sale of *biens* (church land) in small lots and attacked châteaux. The rising in the Midi (Languedoc, Provence and the Rhône valley) in 1792 was as important as any in 1789 in size and the extent of the destruction.

The *sans-culottes* were the workers in the towns. They were not a class, as they included artisans and master craftsmen, who owned their own workshops, as well as wage-earners. They had been responsible for the successful attack on the Bastille and for bringing the royal family back to Paris in the October Days, yet they had received few rewards. Many of them were 'passive' citizens, who did not have the vote. They suffered greatly from inflation. To meet its expenses the government printed more and more assignats, whose value therefore declined. There was a wave of strikes by workers against the falling value of their wages early in 1791. Grain prices rose by up to 50 per cent after a poor harvest in 1791. This resulted in riots, when crowds forced shopkeepers to reduce prices. The discontent of the workers could be used by the popular societies, who linked economic protests to the political demand for a democratic republic, and by groups in the Assembly who were seeking power. This made the Revolution more radical in ways which the bourgeois leaders of 1789 had neither intended nor desired.

4 The Rise of a Republican Movement

> **KEY ISSUE** Why did a republican movement emerge during 1791?

a) The Flight to Varennes

Mirabeau was the outstanding politician and orator in the Constituent Assembly. At the time of his death in April 1791 the moderates were becoming more influential in the Assembly. They feared the new clubs and the emergence of an organised working-class movement. They wanted to end the Revolution but for this to happen there had to be a compromise with the King. This was difficult, as anyone suspected of negotiating with the King would be accused of selling out to the Court. There was also no means of knowing if the King was sincerely prepared to co-operate with the moderates. Louis dashed all their hopes by attempting to flee from Paris. It has been said that the flight was 'the fulcrum (lever) of the Revolution and the test of Louis's character'.[7]

Louis XVI was a devout man, who deeply regretted his acceptance of the Civil Constitution of the Clergy, which offended his conscience. He decided to flee to Montmédy in Lorraine, on the border of Luxembourg, and put himself under the protection of the military commander of the area. He hoped that from there he would be able to renegotiate with the Constituent Assembly the parts of the Constitution he disliked from a position of strength. Military action would, it was hoped, be unnecessary, although the King was aware that there was a danger that his flight might bring about civil war.

Louis left Paris with his family on 20 June 1791. When he reached Varennes, during the night of 21st–22nd, he was recognised by the local postmaster Drouet and stopped. He was brought back to Paris in an atmosphere of deathly silence. Louis' younger brother, the Comte de Provence, was luckier than the King. He also fled from Paris on 20 June with his wife but he arrived safely in Brussels the next day.

Before leaving, Louis had drawn up a proclamation to the French people which set out in great detail his true feelings regarding the developments that had taken place. Writing in the third person he concluded that: 'The king does not think it would be possible to govern so large and important a kingdom as France by the means established by the National Assembly such as they exist at present'.[8] In the declaration it is obvious that Louis had failed to understand the popularity of the changes. What is clear is that once again French people would have to make choices many would have preferred to avoid. Louis had emphatically renounced the revolution. Could he continue to remain as head of state? Support for a republic started to grow. On the 24 June, 30,000 people marched to the National

La famille Des Cochons ramenée Dans L'étable

'The family of pigs brought back to the sty'.

Assembly in support of a petition from the Cordeliers Club calling for the King's deposition (dismissal from office).

One immediate result of the flight was that the King lost what remained of his popularity, which had depended on his being seen to support the Revolution. Royal inn signs and street names disappeared all over Paris. His flight persuaded many who had hitherto supported him that he could no longer be trusted. People started to talk openly of replacing the monarchy with a republic. The deputies in the Assembly acted calmly in this situation. They did not want a republic. They feared that the declaration of a republic would lead to civil war in France and war with European monarchs. Nor did they want to concede victory to the radicals, who wanted more democratic policies. 'Are we going to end the Revolution or are we going to start it again?' one deputy asked the Assembly. On 16 July the Assembly voted to suspend the King until the constitution was completed. Governing without the head of state would encourage those who favored republicanism. He would be restored only after he had sworn to observe it. This was going too far for some deputies – 290 abstained from voting in future as a protest. For others, suspension did not go far enough.

b) The Champ de Mars

Radicals were appalled when the King was not dethroned or put on trial. Their anger was directed against the Assembly, which they claimed no longer represented the people. The Cordeliers took the lead with the popular societies and persuaded the Jacobins to join them in supporting a petition for the King's deposition. This split the

Jacobin Club. Those who did not want the King deposed – and this included nearly all the deputies who were members – left the Club. They set up a new club, the Feuillants, which for the moment had control of the Assembly. Robespierre was left to preside over the more radical rump who remained. It seemed as though the Jacobins had destroyed themselves. However, only 72 of the Jacobin clubs in France defected and most of these drifted back in the next few months.

On 17 July 1791, 50,000 people flocked to the Champ de Mars, a huge field where the Feast of the Federation, celebrating the fall of the Bastille, had been held three days previously. They were there to sign a republican petition on the 'altar of the fatherland'. This was a political demonstration of the poorer sections of the Paris population. The Commune, under pressure from the Assembly, declared martial law. They sent Lafayette with the National Guard to the Champ de Mars, where the Guard fired on the peaceful and unarmed crowd. About 50 people were killed.

This was the first bloody clash between different groups in the Third Estate, and it was greeted with pleasure in the Assembly. Messages of support for the Assembly poured in from the provinces. Martial law remained in force for a month, during which time some popular leaders were arrested. Others, such as Hébert, Marat and Danton fled or went into hiding. The moderates had won – it took nearly a year for the popular movement to recover – and could now work out a compromise with the King without facing mob violence.

The Feuillants were more than ever committed to making an agreement with the King. They did not trust him but they had lost popular support. They controlled Paris and the Assembly for the moment but their long-term success depended on the co-operation of Louis, which was far from certain.

c) The Legislative Assembly

When the King accepted the Constitution in September 1791, the Constituent Assembly was dissolved. By this time, suspicion and hatred amongst the deputies had replaced the euphoria of 1789. This change had come about because of the King's reluctance to accept measures he disliked and because of the fear of counter-revolutionary plots. To prevent his opponents from dominating the next Assembly, Robespierre proposed a self-denying ordinance, which was passed, that no member of the Constituent Assembly could sit in the next Legislative Assembly. In the ensuing elections under a quarter of the 'active' citizens voted. They elected an Assembly of 745 members which was almost wholly bourgeois. There were few nobles, most of whom retired to their estates and kept a low profile, hoping for better times. Only 23 clergy were elected. There were no peasants nor artisans, and few businessmen. At the beginning, 264 deputies were members of the Feuillant Club, who considered the Revolution to be over, and 136 deputies were members of the Jacobin Club. The majority of deputies (345) were unattached.

The deputies were worried by the non-juring clergy and by the émigrés, whose numbers had increased greatly since the flight to Varennes. Nearly all the *ancien régime* bishops and many of the great court and *parlementaire* families had emigrated. What alarmed the Assembly most was the desertion of army officers. By early 1791, 1,200 noble officers had joined the *émigrés*, though a large majority of pre-Revolution officers remained at their posts. All this changed after Varennes. By the end of 1791, about 6,000 had emigrated, 60 per cent of all officers. The Assembly passed two laws in November. One declared that all non-jurors were suspects. The other said that all émigrés who did not return to France by 1 January 1792 would forfeit their property and be regarded as traitors. When the King vetoed these laws his unpopularity increased. He appeared to be undermining the Revolution.

Yet in spite of the mistrust of the King, it seemed likely that the Constitution of 1791 would survive. What prevented this was the outbreak of war with Austria in April 1792. This event had more decisive and far-reaching results than any other in the whole of the Revolution. Almost everything that happened in France from that time was caused, or was affected, by it. The war finally destroyed the consensus of 1789. It led directly to the fall of the monarchy, to civil war and to the Terror.

5 The Outbreak of War

> **KEY ISSUE** Why did France go to war in April 1792?

The Great Powers had shown no inclination to intervene during the first two years of the French Revolution. Leopold II, the Habsburg Emperor, approved of many of the liberal reforms in the Revolution and did not want a return to absolutism in France. He, like other sovereigns, was pleased at the collapse of French power and no longer regarded France as a serious rival. In any case, Russia, Austria and Prussia were occupied elsewhere. From 1787, Russia and Austria were at war with the Ottoman Empire. Leopold abandoned the fight in July 1790 to concentrate on the Austrian Netherlands (Belgium), where there was a revolt. He crushed this in the winter of 1790 and then turned his attention to Poland, where Russia and Prussia were seeking to gain territory. All three powers were more interested in what was happening in Poland than in what was going on in France.

After the flight to Varennes, the Austrians felt they had to make some gesture in support of Louis. In August 1791, they issued the Declaration of Pillnitz in association with Prussia. This said that they were ready with the other sovereigns of Europe to restore the King of

France to a position from which he could strengthen the foundations of monarchical government. This appeared to be a threat to interfere in French internal affairs, but, in reality, it was no threat at all. The Austrians knew that the other powers, such as Britain, would not join them. This meant that the Declaration would not lead to any action. In France the Declaration did not create much of a stir. The Assembly did not debate it and most newspapers ignored it. When the Constitution was passed in September, Leopold gave it a warm welcome, so the possibility of Austrian intervention was even more remote.

In France, several people, for very different reasons, came to believe that war was either in their own best interests or in those of France. Marie Antoinette ('the only man in the family', Mirabeau called her) wrote to her brother, the Emperor Leopold II, in September 1791: 'Conciliation is out of the question now. Armed force has destroyed everything and only armed force can put things right'. She hoped for a war in which France would be defeated, enabling Louis to recover his old powers. The King shared her view that France would be defeated. 'The physical condition and morale of France', he wrote, 'is such that it will be unable to sustain even half a campaign.' At the same time as he was taking an oath to defend the Constitution, the Queen was writing to the Austrian ambassador: 'giving the impression of adopting the new ideas is the safest way of quickly defeating them'. The deputies were not taken in. Rumours abounded that the country's foreign policy was being run by an 'Austrian Committee', headed by Marie Antoinette, and that secret agents were being sent to Koblenz (the headquarters of the *émigrés*) and Vienna to plot counter-revolution. These rumours were well founded.

Army commanders such as Lafayette and Dumouriez also wanted war. Lafayette, the first commander of the National Guard, had brought the King from Versailles to Paris during the October Days and was responsible for the 'massacre' of the Champ de Mars. He had become disillusioned by the failure of the Revolution to produce political stability and wanted the authority of the King to be strengthened. This could be done by waging a short, successful war against Austria, which would increase his prestige as a general. It would also enable him to dictate his own terms to both the King and the Assembly.

The desire for war resulted in the co-operation of Lafayette and his followers with the Brissotins, who also wanted war. The Brissotins were not a party, but a group of deputies led by Jacques Brissot. They merged with some deputies from the Gironde department in south-western France and so were also known as Girondins. Brissot was one of the first to support a republic and after the flight from Varennes he argued for the abolition of the monarchy and the trial of Louis XVI. He saw that the King had not really accepted the Constitution and that the Court was plotting against the Revolution and seeking the armed intervention of the European powers. A war would force the King to come out into the open, as it would expose traitors and those who were opposed to the Revolution.

There were about 130 Girondins in the Assembly, so to obtain a majority they needed the support both of Lafayette and his followers and of the unorganised centre. Brissot obtained this by playing on their hopes and fears in a campaign for war which he began in October 1791. He maintained that a successful war would rouse enthusiasm for the Revolution and show the permanence of the new regime. In a war the appeal of revolutionary ideals abroad would be irresistible and French armies would have the active support of the enemy's own repressed subjects. Brissot thought that the international situation was promising for France. The European powers would not unite against France because Britain would not join in, Russia was preoccupied with Poland and Prussia was more likely to fight for France than against her.

Most deputies were won over by these arguments but some politicians outside the Assembly, particularly Robespierre, were not. He made known his impassioned opposition to war in the Jacobin Club. 'You propose to give supreme power to those who most want your ruin', he said. 'The only way to save the state and to safeguard freedom is to wage war in the right way, on our enemies at home, instead of marching under their orders against their allies across the frontiers.' The real threat, therefore, came from soldiers like Lafayette, who were still popular enough to mislead the public. He saw that the European powers aimed at intimidating France, not invading her. War would be more difficult than Brissot expected, because foreigners would not rise up in support of French invaders: 'no one loves armed missionaries.' Robespierre became isolated and unpopular and was convinced that his opponents were plotting to betray the Revolution. His relations with Brissot were poisoned by bitter personal quarrels and the suspicion of each other's motives which underlay them.

The Girondins were pressing hard for war but it is doubtful whether they would have gained the support of the majority of deputies without the bungling of Austria and Prussia. On 7 February 1792 Prussia and Austria became allies and thought they could intimidate the French by threatening war. They had great confidence in their own armies: in 1789 a small Prussian army had conquered the United Provinces in under a month. In 1790 a small Austrian army occupied Belgium in under two weeks. They believed France to be weak from civil war and mutinies in the army as well as bankrupt. She would have neither the will nor the ability to resist Austrian pressure.

Austrian threats and Girondin attacks on the 'Austrian Committee' at Court forced the King to dismiss his Feuillant ministers in March 1792 and to appoint a more radical government, including some

Girondin ministers. This was a decisive change. The old ministers had carried out the wishes of the King: the new ones obeyed the Assembly. Both the Assembly and the government now wanted war, especially the new Foreign Minister, General Dumouriez. He hated Austria but had aims similar to those of Lafayette: a short successful war would increase his own personal power and that of the Crown. In Austria the pacific Leopold had died on 1 March and had been replaced by the young and impetuous Francis II. Austria decided, reluctantly, on war when there were rumours that Marie Antoinette was to be put on trial. But it was the French who actually declared war, on 20 April 1792. Only seven deputies voted against it. The French hoped to fight solely against Austria but Prussia declared war on France a month later and took the lead in the campaign, with the Duke of Brunswick as commander-in-chief. For very different reasons, influential groups in the Assembly and supporters of the King decided, that war would serve their interests best. They hoped for a short decisive war. The resulting conflict lasted nine years, lost France 1.4 million of her inhabitants and dramatically altered the trajectory of the revolution.[9]

6 The Overthrow of the Monarchy

> **KEY ISSUE** Why was the Monarchy overthrown in the summer of 1792?

When war was declared, the French army was not well prepared. Of its 12,000 officers half had emigrated. The army's strength was also depleted. There were 150,000 men under arms in 1791 comprising both regular and newly recruited volunteers. A combination of desertion and revolutionary propaganda had destroyed the discipline of the regular army, while the volunteers were poorly trained and equipped. The French advanced into the Austrian Netherlands and were defeated on 20 April. The soldiers of the French army panicked and retreated headlong to Lille, where they murdered their commander. Whole units deserted. By the end of May all three field commanders were advising that peace should be made immediately. Allied armies invaded France. Treason and traitors were blamed for French defeats and with some justification: Marie Antoinette had sent details of French military plans to the Austrians.

The government also had other problems to cope with, such as opposition from non-juring priests and counter-revolutionaries. The Girondins had to satisfy the popular clamour for action against 'traitors'. On 27 May the Assembly passed a law for the deportation of refractory priests. Another law disbanded the King's Guard and a third set up a camp for 20,000 National Guards (they were known as *fédérés* because their arrival was to coincide with the Feast of the Federation on 14 July) from the provinces. They were to protect Paris from invasion and the government from a coup by the generals, especially Lafayette. Louis refused to approve these laws. When Roland, the Girondin Minister of the Interior, protested, Louis dismissed him and other Girondin ministers on 13 June. Dumouriez resigned soon afterwards. On 19 June Louis vetoed the laws on refractory priests and the *fédéré* camp.

People expected a military coup when a letter from Lafayette was read out in the Assembly on 18 June. He accused the Jacobins of setting up a state within the state and demanded that the Assembly should end the rule of the clubs. Napoleon Bonaparte observed how France was dividing:

1 M. De Lafayette has written to the National Assembly denouncing the Jacobins. His letter is very strongly expressed . . . M. De Lafayette, the majority of officers in the army, all honest men, the ministers and the Parisian administration are on one side; on the other are most of
5 the Assembly, the Jacobins and the people.

Leaders of the Sections (Paris had been divided into 48 sections to replace the 60 electoral districts of 1789) responded to these events by holding an armed demonstration on 20 June, the anniversary of the Tennis Court Oath and of the flight to Varennes. Their leaders came from the Cordeliers Club. The Jacobins stayed aloof, as they had done at the time of the Champ de Mars petition. About 8,000 demonstrators, many of them National Guards, poured into the Tuileries. One participant described what happened, when he reported to the Jacobin Club:

1 I have just come from the Tuileries where, at a window, I saw the King wearing a red cap . . . He was sitting on a slightly raised seat with three or four national Guards and a few deputies at his side. The people had entered this apartment in considerable numbers, shouting: 'Down with
5 the veto! Ratify the decrees! Long live the nation!' The King was wearing the cap of liberty on his head and was drinking from a bottle, to the health of the nation. He was unable to make himself heard and several times he rang a little bell to get them to listen. When he finally got their attention he told them that he was in favour of the Constitution and
10 swore to uphold it. The people shouted that it wasn't true, that he had already deceived them and would do so again and then they went on: 'Bring back the patriot ministers!'

Louis behaved with great dignity. He was not intimidated and his calmness may have saved his life. This *journée* did not achieve its desired end: the King did not withdraw his veto or recall the Girondin ministers. However, it did show very clearly the weakness of the King and the Assembly and the power of the Sections.

The Assembly soon took steps which recognised the growing importance of the *sans-culottes* but which also increased the likelihood of a rising. On 11 July it declared a state of emergency by issuing a decree '*la patrie en danger*' (the fatherland in danger), which called on every Frenchman to fight. This tilted the balance of power in favour of the democrats. How could you ask a man to fight and not give him a vote? The Sections, whose assemblies were allowed to meet in permanent session, and *fédérés* demanded the admission of 'passive' citizens into the sectional assemblies and National Guard, requests which were granted by the end of the month. The middle-class control of 1789 gave way to the popular democracy of the *sans-culottes*.

Tension in Paris was increased by the arrival of *fédérés* from the provinces and by the publication of the Brunswick Manifesto (see below). The *fédérés* were militant revolutionaries and republicans, unlike the Paris National Guard, whose officers were conservative or royalist. Their patriotism was expressed in the war song of the Rhine army, composed in Strasbourg by Rouget de Lisle. It acquired its name '*La Marseillaise*' as it was sung by the *fédérés* of Marseille on their march to the capital. In July their total number in Paris was never above 5,000 but they were a powerful pressure group in the radical sections, calling for the removal of the King.

The Brunswick Manifesto, issued by the commander-in-chief of the Austro-Prussian armies, was published in Paris on 1 August. It threatened that any National Guards captured fighting would be punished 'as rebels to their King'. Parisians were collectively held responsible for the safety of the royal family. If it was harmed the allies would execute 'an exemplary vengeance . . . by delivering the city of Paris to a military execution'. The Manifesto was intended to help the King but it had the opposite effect. Frenchmen were infuriated and many who had supported the monarchy now turned against it.

As a new insurrection was being prepared by radicals and *fédérés* from the middle of July, the Girondins changed their attitude of opposition to the King and tried to prevent a rising. They warned the King that there was likely to be a more violent uprising than that of 20 June and that he would, at least, be deposed. They offered to do all they could to prevent such an uprising, if he would recall the ministers dismissed on 13 June. Louis haughtily rejected their offer. Meanwhile, the Jacobin leader Robespierre was co-operating with the central committee of the *fédérés* and on 29 July, in a speech to the Jacobin Club, he put forward his proposals. He abandoned his previous support for the Constitution of 1791 and called for the overthrow of the monarchy. He also wanted a National Convention, elected by universal male suffrage to replace the Legislative Assembly, and a purge of the departmental authorities, many of which were royalist. Hitherto he had warned the *fédérés* and the Sections against precipitate action, as this might lead to a backlash in the King's favour. Now he felt the moment had come to strike. Petitions were pouring in from the *fédérés*, the clubs and provinces for the removal of the King. On 3 August Pétion, the Mayor of Paris, went to the

Legislative Assembly and demanded, on behalf of 47 out of the 48 Sections, the abolition of the monarchy. Yet the Assembly refused to depose the King and defeated a motion to put Lafayette on trial. This finally persuaded many that a rising was necessary.

On the night of 9 August *sans-culottes* took over the Hôtel de Ville, overthrew the old municipality and set up a revolutionary Commune. Typical of its leaders was Hébert, who had taken part in the Cordeliers agitation of the last year and had strong links with the Sections and the *fédérés*. The next morning several thousand of the National Guard, which was now open to 'passive citizens', and 2,000 *fédérés*, led by those from Marseille, marched on the Tuileries. The palace was defended by 3,000 troops, 2,000 of whom were National Guards. The others were Swiss mercenaries who were certain to resist. During the morning the King sought refuge in the Assembly to protect his family. The National Guard defending the Tuileries joined the insurgents, who entered the courtyards. They believed the attack was over until the Swiss began to fire. The *Marseillais* replied with grapeshot and it seemed that a violent battle was about to take place. At this point the King ordered his Swiss guards to cease fire. This left them at the mercy of the attackers: 600 Swiss were massacred. Of the insurgents, 90 *fédérés* and 300 Parisians (tradesmen, craftsmen, wage-earners) had been killed or wounded. It was the bloodiest *journée* of the Revolution.

The rising was as much a rejection of the Assembly as it was of the King. The insurgents invaded the Assembly and forced it to recognise the new revolutionary Commune, which had given the orders for the attack on the palace. The deputies had to hand over the King to the Commune, who imprisoned him in the Temple. They also had to agree to the election, by universal male suffrage, of a National Convention to draw up a new, democratic constitution. The Commune was now in control in Paris, though in the rest of France it was the authority of the Assembly alone that was recognised.

The constitutional monarchists, about two-thirds of the deputies, did not feel safe, so they stayed away from the Assembly and went into hiding. This left the Girondins in charge, the beneficiaries of a revolution they had tried to avoid. The 300 deputies remaining in the Assembly appointed new ministers, including the three who had been dismissed earlier. A surprise appointment was that of Danton. He made his career in the Cordeliers Club and the Paris Sections and now became Minister of Justice to please the *sans-culottes*. In its final six weeks, the Assembly did all that the Commune wanted. It passed several radical measures, including the deportation of refractory priests. Peasant support was necessary after 10 August, as many provinces resented this latest attack on the monarchy. The Assembly decreed that redeemable feudal dues were abolished without compensation, unless the *seigneur* could produce the title-deeds. This effectively ended the feudal regime, which peasants had unsuccessfully been trying to do since the August Decrees of 1789. The

Assembly also ordered that *émigré* lands should be sold in small lots. The King was suspended: it was left for the Convention to decide whether or not to dethrone him.

The Convention met for the first time on 20 September 1792. There was little doubt that Louis would be deposed. Royal documents found in the Tuileries after the 10 August confirmed what was widely suspected – that the King had behaved treacherously. On 21 September the monarchy in France was abolished.

References

1   George Rudé, *The French Revolution* (Weidenfeld and Nicolson,1988) p. 60.
2   P.M. Jones, *The Peasantry in the French Revolution* (Cambridge, 1988) p. 155.
3   Georges Lefebvre, *Les Paysans du nord la Révolution Française* (Bari, 1959) pp. 431–525.
4   Albert Soboul, op. cit. p. 191.
5   Nigel Aston, *Religion and Revolution in France 1780–1804* (Macmillan, 2000) p. 162.
6   Emmet Kennedy, *A Cultural History of the French Revolution* (Yale, 1989) p. 366.
7   John Hardman, *Louis XVI* (Arnold, 2000) p. 115.
8   John Hardman, *The French Revolution. The fall of the Ancien Régime to the Thermidorian reaction 1785–1797* (Arnold, 1981) pp. 124–134 for the full text.
9   T.C.W. Blanning, *The Origins of The French Revolutionary Wars* (Longman, 1986) Chapter 3.

Working on Chapter 3

This chapter covers a great deal of information relating to how the revolution affected the population in the initial phase, and how the king and leading figures reacted to these changes. You need to understand why the experiment in establishing a constitutional monarchy failed and gave way to republicanism. To help you understand how these changes occurred you may find it useful to keep in mind the following questions: **i)** what was the reaction of the King to the revolution? **ii)** what factors contributed to the rise of republicanism? **iii)** How did the war contribute to the overthrow of the monarchy? It is possible that in an examination you may be asked how France was changed as a result of the reform programme. Read carefully section 2 and try and draw up a list of the key reforms, note who they benefited and how they differed from the *ancien régime*.

Answering structured and essay questions on Chapter 3

There are many opportunities within the content of this chapter for an examiner to ask structured questions. Consider the following examples:

1   a) Explain briefly the main features of the constitution of 1791? (*8 marks*)
    b) To what extent did the reforms of the Legislative assembly improve the lives of ordinary citizens in France? (*12 marks*)
2   a) Explain briefly the reasons why France went to war in 1792? (*8 marks*)
    b) How important a factor in the overthrow of Louis XVI was the outbreak of the war? (*12 marks*)

With essay questions you will be required to be selective in the use of the material available to you. The questions will be phrased in such a way that your response will need to be a considered, balanced, judgement which is presented in the form of an argument. It may well be that the examiner provides a provocative quotation which while accurate in some ways, is also selective and omits other factors. The best responses are based on a good mastery of the relevant detail, while never becoming narrative or chronological accounts. Remember to keep referring to the question in your answer. Study the following questions:

1   To what extent did the reforms of Constituent Assembly reshape France?

Whenever an examiner uses the phrase 'to what extent' he/she wants the candidate to engage in a balanced evaluation of the question. You will need to cover the central reforms undertaken by the Constituent Assembly (section 2) but avoid adopting a narrative approach. Did the reforms fail to tackle any areas? You should consider the bourgeois nature of the changes, which failed to satisfy many workers and peasants.

2   'Why did the attempts to create a limited monarchy in France between 1789 and 1792 fail?'

Draw up a list of reasons for (causes of) the fall of the monarchy. These may include: the character and actions of the King; divisions within the Assembly; fear of counter-revolution; the actions of revolutionary clubs; the discontent of the *sans-culottes*; the opening of the National Guard to 'passive' citizens; the war and initial defeats. When you have made your list, do not treat all the causes as of equal importance. Try to produce a hierarchy of causes. Was there one cause, above all others, which led to the downfall of the monarchy?

Answering Source-based questions on Chapter 3

1 The Declaration of the Rights of Man and the Citizen

Read carefully the extracts from the Declaration on page 38 and then answer the following questions:

a) Explain briefly the reference to '... sovereignty resides in the nation' (lines 6–7)? (*4 marks*)

b) In what ways did the Declaration reinforce the liberty of the individual? (*6 marks*)

c) To what extent did the Declaration reflect the interests of the bourgeoisie? (*8 marks*)

d) How useful is the source in understanding the limitations imposed by the *ancien régime*? (*10 marks*)

2 The Civil Constitution of the Clergy

Read carefully the extract from the Civil Constitution of the Clergy on page 46 and then answer the following questions:

a) Explain briefly the reference '. . . bishop whose see is established under the control of a foreign power' (lines 5–6). (*4 marks*)

b) In what ways did the constitution limit papal power in France? (*6 marks*)

c) To what extent did the constitution propose to make the church accountable to the people? (*8 marks*)

d) How useful is the source in understanding the causes of the division between the Catholic church and the French state? (*10 marks*)

4 War and Revolt: 1792–3

POINTS TO CONSIDER

This chapter deals with the war between France and her neighbouring European states. The war was to have a decisive impact upon the course of the revolution. You will need to understand the consequences of the early years of the war on France and note carefully the internal, as well as the external, impact. Why did a defensive war become a war of conquest? Pay close attention to the power struggle in the National Convention between the Jacobin and the Girondin and the emergence of a more authoritarian and centralised government.

KEY DATES

1792	**Apr**	War declared on Austria (20th)
	Jun	Prussia declared war on France(13th)
	Aug	Prussian forces entered northern France (19th), fall of Longwy (20th)
	Sept	Fall of Verdun (2nd), 'September Massacres' (2nd–6th), Valmy (20th)
		Convention met (21st), Republic proclaimed (22nd)
	Nov	Battle of Jemappes (6th), Decree of Fraternity (19th)
1793	**Jan**	Louis XVI executed (21st)
	Feb	War declared on Great Britain and the Dutch Republic (1st)
	Mar	Revolt in the Vendée (11th)
	Apr	Committee of Public safety created (6th)
		Federalist uprising started – Marseilles (29th)
	Jun	Purge of the Girondin deputies (2nd)
	Jul	Marat assassinated

1 The Republic at War

> **KEY ISSUES** Why did the republic embark on a war of conquest? What were the differences between the Girondin and the Jacobin?

a) Defeat and Crisis – The September Massacres

In the summer of 1793 the situation of the French armies on the frontier was desperate. Lafayette fled to the Austrians on 17 August. With a leading general deserting, who could still be trusted? Panic and fear of treachery swept the country. This was

increased when the Prussians crossed the French frontier and captured Longwy. By the beginning of September, Verdun, the last
major fortress on the road to Paris, was about to surrender. The
French capital was under serious threat, and the revolution itself
was in danger of being overthrown.

In this desperate situation the forces of nationalism and patriotism
were summoned. The Commune called on all patriots to take up
arms. Thousands volunteered to defend the capital and the
Revolution. But, once they had left for the front, there was growing
concern about the overcrowded prisons, which contained many
priests and nobles as counter-revolutionary suspects. A rumour arose
that these were plotting to escape, kill the helpless population and
hand the city over to the Prussians. Marat, a powerful figure in the
Commune, called for the conspirators to be killed. The massacre of
prisoners was the first appearance of the terror. It began on 2
September and continued for five days. Between 1,100 and 1,400 of
the 2,600 prisoners in Paris jails were murdered. Only a quarter were

Contemporary print showing the September Massacres 1793

priests and nobles: the rest were common criminals. The killers were the *sans-culottes* of the Sections. The Commune made no attempt to stop them, neither did Danton, the Minister of Justice. This would have meant mobilising the National Guard and risking another Champ de Mars.

The massacre cast a shadow over the first meeting of the Convention. Most deputies from the provinces were shocked by the killings and rallied to the Girondins. The hatred of the Girondins for the Jacobins and for their *sans-culotte* supporters was intensified. From now on, moderates and foreign opinion regarded Montagnards and *sans-culottes* as bloodthirsty savages – *buveurs de sang* (drinkers of blood).

Just as the fortunes of war had brought about the September Massacres, they also brought an end to this first phase of the Terror. On 20 September at Valmy 52,000 French troops defeated 34,000 Prussians. This was a very significant victory. If the Prussians had won, there is little doubt that Paris would have fallen. This would probably have meant the end of the Revolution. The new forces summoned by the decree of 12 July 1792 were very effective, par- ticularly as they were supplemented by many volunteers, and National Guardsmen. In the main, these men were workers and traders who belonged to the *sans culottes* rather than being the sons of the bourgeoisie. Their commitment to the revolutionary cause was likely to be considerable. Following the Prussian defeat Goethe wrote 'This day and this place open a new era in the history of the world'.

Brunswick, the Prussian commander-in-chief, retreated to the frontier. The French republic would not be easily defeated. French armies once again took the offensive. Within a month they had occupied much of the left bank of the Rhine. In November, Dumouriez defeated the Austrians at Jemappes and occupied most of Belgium. This was the first major battle won by Republican forces.

The French now began to talk about expanding to reach their natural frontiers, the Rhine, Alps and Pyrenees, which meant annex- ing territory. This was contrary to the policy laid down by the Constituent Assembly in May 1790: 'the French nation renounces involvement in any war undertaken with the aim of making con- quest'. The change in policy was accompanied by propaganda. On 19 November 1792 the Convention promised '. . . to extend fraternal feelings and aid to all peoples who may wish to regain their liberty.' Some politicians were attracted to the prospect of extending the rev- olution to other states. Brissot wrote 'We can only be at peace once Europe . . . is blazing from end to end'. As long as France was under threat from hostile monarchs there would be little prospect of secur- ity. But, if these monarchs could be defeated, the Republic would sur- vive. Avignon, papal territory in France since 1273, had been annexed in 1791. Now Savoy (November 1792) and Nice (January 1793) were added to French territory. A revolutionary administration was set up in conquered lands. French armies had to be paid and fed at the expense of the local population. Church lands and those belonging to enemies of the new regime were confiscated. Tithes and feudal dues were abolished. Everyone did not support these measures which alienated many of the population, and confirmed Robespierre's prediction that French armies would not be welcomed abroad.

b) The Power Struggle in the Convention: Girondins and Jacobins

All men over 21 could vote in the elections to the Convention, which were held at the end of August and the beginning of September 1792, but the result was distorted by fear and intimidation. In Paris, all who had shown royalist sympathies were disfranchised. Thus, all 24 members for Paris were Jacobins, republicans and supporters of the Commune. Robespierre came head of the poll in the capital. At first there were about 200 Girondins and 100 Jacobins in the Convention. The majority of deputies, uncommitted to either group, were known as the 'Plain' or 'Marsh' because of the middle ground where they sat in the Assembly. About a third of the deputies were lawyers. The proportion representing business and trade had declined to nine per cent (compared with 13 per cent in the Constituent Assembly).

Until 2 June 1793 the history of the Convention was that of a struggle between the Girondins and Jacobins. The latter came to be known as the Montagnards or 'the Mountain' or simply the Left, because they sat on the upper benches of the Assembly to the left of the President's chair. This is a better name for them than Jacobins, as the Girondins too were members of the Jacobin Club, where both groups argued fiercely with one another. Neither group was a party which had an agreed programme or accepted a common discipline. People disapproved of parties, which were regarded as pursuing the selfish interests of the members rather than the common good, very much like the corporations and guilds of the old regime had done. It is, therefore, very difficult to say how many deputies belonged to each group at any time.

The Girondins and Montagnards were all bourgeois and agreed on most policies. Both believed strongly in the Revolution and the Republic, hated privilege, were anti-clerical and favoured a liberal economic policy. Both wanted a more enlightened and humane France. However, they differed in the sources of their support and in their deep suspicions of each other. The Girondins had most of the Paris press on their side and had much support in the provinces, though it must be remembered that most Montagnard deputies were also from the provinces. However, the opposition of many Girondins to the *journée* of 10 August lost them the support of the Paris militants. The Montagnards, weaker in the provinces than the Girondins, had the solid backing of the clubs and Sections in Paris. They emerged, therefore, as the main champions of Paris as the centre of the Revolution. The Girondins, on the other hand, supported federalism: the right of the provinces to run their own affairs without interference from Paris. This was very similar to the policy of the Constituent Assembly from 1789 to 1791. Both Girondins and Montagnards were committed to winning the war but the latter were more flexible in their approach. They realised that the support of the people was needed for military victory and that therefore some of their demands would have to be met. The Girondins thought that Robespierre wanted a bloody dictatorship: the Montagnards were convinced that the Girondins would seek arrangements with conservative, even royalist, forces to stay in power. Therefore, they accused them of supporting counter-revolution.

As neither side had a majority in the Assembly, each needed to have the support of the Plain. They too were bourgeois, believed in economic liberalism and were deeply afraid of the popular movement. At first they supported the Girondins, who provided most of the ministers and dominated most of the Assembly's committees.

c) The Trial of Louis XVI

The Jacobins insisted on the trial of the King, in order to establish the republic more firmly. They increasingly depended on the *sans-culottes*, who wanted the King tried and executed, as they held him responsible for the bloodshed at the Tuileries in August 1792. The Girondins tried to prevent a trial and, when they were not able to do this, they made two attempts to save Louis' life. They proposed that a referendum should be held to decide the King's fate. When the King was found guilty and sentenced to death, they proposed a reprieve.

Two factors sealed the King's fate. The first was the discovery of a secret iron chest (the *armoire de fer*) containing incriminating royal correspondence with Austria. Cobban suggests that this 'was the death warrant of Louis XVI'.[1] The second was Marat's proposal that a decision should be reached by '*appel nominal*' (each deputy was to announce his decision publicly), 'so that traitors in this Assembly may be known'. In an Assembly of 721 deputies, no one voted that Louis was innocent, while 693 voted that he was guilty. When it came to the sentence 361 voted unconditionally for the death penalty, and 319 for imprisonment. The Convention voted against a reprieve by 387 votes to 334. 'The voting in the trial had revealed for all to see a solid bloc of moderates,'[2] who were reluctant to support the execution of the King.

The King was executed on 21 January 1793. As Saint-Just, a leading Jacobin, said, he was executed not for what he had done but for what he was: a menace to the Republic. A recent biographer of Louis XVI

The Execution of Louis XVI in the place de la revolution, January 1793

has written that his main handicap in the period after 1789 was that he was not trusted, a view apparently confirmed by the discovery of the *armoire de fer*.[3] It was the first Jacobin victory in the Convention and left the factions more hostile to one another than ever. Although over half the Girondin leaders, including Brissot, had voted for the death penalty, they were branded as royalists and counter-revolutionaries by the Montagnards. By Louis' execution the Montagnards gained an ascendancy in the Convention which they rarely lost afterwards. Brissot hardly spoke there after the trial.

d) The War Extended – The War of the First Coalition

The Convention threatened the European monarchs with its Edict of Fraternity. In January 1793 it passed a decree claiming for France the natural frontiers of the Rhine, Alps and Pyrenees. The Great Powers were alarmed at the annexation of Nice and Savoy and Britain was particularly concerned at the Rhine becoming a natural frontier for France. This would involve the annexation of a large part of the United Provinces as well as the whole of Belgium. William Pitt, the British Prime Minister, was determined that both of these should be kept out of French hands. They were seen as the key to British security, not only in the Channel but also on the routes to India (as the Dutch possessed the Cape of Good Hope and Ceylon). The British also disliked the French re-opening the River Scheldt to navigation (its closure since 1648 had led to the decline of the port of Antwerp as a rival to London).

The French misunderstood the situation in Britain. They did not realise that the reform movement there was not revolutionary. They mistakenly thought that there would be a revolution in Britain. They also thought that in war Britain would crumble as Prussia and Austria had done at Valmy and Jemappes. The British, for their part, thought that France was bankrupt and on the verge of civil war. Each side thought the war would be short and easy and entered into it lightly. The Convention unanimously declared war on Britain and Holland in February 1793, and on Spain in March. With the exception of Switzerland and the Baltic states, France was at war with the whole of Europe. The first coalition emerged slowly between March and September 1793. Britain was the driving force binding the other powers together as there was no formal treaty. Her diplomacy persuaded Russia, Sardinia, Portugal and Naples to join the anti-French crusade.

The campaign in 1793 began very badly for the French. Their armies had lost their numerical superiority of the previous year and morale was low. An attack against Holland failed and the French commander, Dumouriez, was defeated by the Austrians at Neerwinden in March. He reached an agreement with the Austrian commander and planned to march on Paris, dissolve the Convention and restore the Constitution of 1791 and the monarchy. When his army refused to follow him, he deserted to the Austrians along with the Duc de Chartres – the future King Louis Philippe, son of the Duc d'Orléans (Philippe Égalité). The defection of Dumouriez, who had enjoyed the enthusiastic backing of the Girondins, further weakened the Girondins' position in the Convention and within the Paris clubs. Meanwhile, the French lost Belgium and the left bank of the Rhine and there was fighting once again on French soil. Leading figures such as Danton were urging conciliation with the coalition. With the military situation deteriorating rapidly a large rebellion broke out in the Vendée.

2 The Revolt in the Provinces

KEY ISSUE Why did the Vendée rebel against the republican government?

a) The Vendée Rebellion

By the winter of 1792–3 the counter-revolution in France had virtually collapsed. To view the Vendée uprising as a revival of this, is perhaps to oversimplify the analysis. As James Roberts argues it may be more appropriate to describe it as 'anti-revolution' rather than 'counter-revolution' in that it was directed against the revolution and its demands rather than for restoring the *ancien régime*.[4] The catalyst for the uprising was the expansion of the war and conscription. The government ordered a levy of 300,000 troops in February 1793. This led to a massive uprising in four departments south of the Loire in what became known as the '*Vendée militaire*' or simply the Vendée. The troubles in the Vendée had begun long before 1793 and conscription. Peasants there were paying more in land tax than they had under the *ancien régime* and so disliked the revolutionary government. This dislike turned into hatred with the Civil Constitution of the Clergy (see pages 45–7). It had been strongly resisted in the area and there were many non-jurors. A local inhabitant of the Vendée writing in March 1793 explained some of the issues involved in the rebellion:

1 Gentlemen and brothers. On Monday 11th of the month the rebel bands began to assemble. The young men simply wanted to hold an assembly to agree not to send men to the national army. In addition the decree on religious freedom is one of the principles of the revolt, 5 because the people consider that to give them priests whom they do not want is a denial of freedom.[5]

The sale of church lands was also unpopular, because most were bought by the bourgeoisie of the towns, who often raised rents. Those who bought *biens* became supporters of the Revolution, which was a guarantee they could keep the land. Those who were not successful became hostile to the government. The peasants looked to the nobles as their natural leaders. Many of these were monarchist, so the rising became caught up in counter-revolution. New local officials, constitutional priests and National Guards were massacred. The situation was so serious that in May the government had to withdraw 30,000 troops from the front to deal with the rising. Yet the rebels were never a serious threat to the government in Paris. They were ill-disciplined – better at guerrilla warfare than set-piece battles – and unwilling to move far from their homes.

Economic problems, for which the war was largely responsible, added to the difficulties of the government. To pay for the war more and more assignats were printed and they had fallen to half their nominal value by February 1793. This pushed up prices. The harvest in 1792 was good but bread was scarce. Saint-Just pointed out why in a speech in November 1792: 'The farmer does not want to save paper money and for this reason he is most reluctant to sell his grain'. The results of high prices and scarcity were, as usual, widespread riots and demands from the *sans-culottes* for price controls and requisitioning.

The support of the people was necessary to fight the war, so it was clear that some of their demands would have to be granted. This was realised first of all by the Montagnards. And just as the Montagnards were drawing closer to the *sans-culottes*, the Plain was drawing closer to the Montagnards. Its members shared the Girondin hatred of Robespierre and Marat, but they held the Girondins responsible for the failures in the war (Dumouriez had been closely associated with them), the rising in the Vendée and the economic crisis. After all, several ministers were Girondins. The Plain, therefore, joined the Montagnards in favour of repressive measures. Barère, a leader of the Plain, told the Convention that it should recognise three things: in a state of emergency no government could rule by normal methods; the bourgeoisie should not isolate itself from the people, whose demands should be satisfied; the bourgeoisie must retain control of this alliance, and so the Convention must take the initiative by introducing the necessary measures.

These measures were passed by the Convention between 10 March and 20 May 1793. They had three objectives: to watch and punish suspects, to make government more effective and to meet at least some of the economic demands of the *sans-culottes*. On 10 March a Revolutionary Tribunal was set up in Paris to try counter-revolutionary suspects and was intended to prevent massacres like those of September 1792. 'Let us embody Terror', said Danton in the debate on the decree, 'so as to prevent the people from doing so'. This tribunal was to become one of the main agencies of the Terror.

Owing to the resistance to conscription and the suspicion of generals after Dumouriez's defection, representatives-on-mission were sent to the provinces. They had almost unlimited powers over the department administrations and the armies. They were deputies of the Convention, mainly Montagnards, whose job was to speed up conscription and keep an eye on the conduct of generals, whom they could arrest. This was the first stage in reasserting central control over the provinces, which had been dismantled in the local government reforms.

Plots were blamed for the rising in the Vendée, so *comités de surveillance* (surveillance or watch committees, sometimes known simply as revolutionary committees) were set up in each commune and each section of major towns. They were to keep an eye on foreigners and suspected traitors, and they provided many victims for the Revolutionary Tribunal. Severe measures were to be taken against rebels. The summary execution decree provided for the trial and execution of armed rebels within 24 hours of capture. These trials were held without a jury and there was no appeal. They condemned many more victims than the Revolutionary Tribunal itself. Very harsh laws were also passed against *émigrés*. Their property was confiscated and they were to be executed if they returned to France.

On 6 April perhaps the most important of all these measures, the Committee of Public Safety was set up to supervise and speed up the activities of ministers, whose authority it superseded. The Committee was not a dictatorship: it depended on the support of the convention, which renewed its powers each month. Who was to be on the new Committee? Danton, supported by the Plain, wanted a committee without extremists. Thus of the nine members selected in April, seven, including Barère, were from the Plain. There were only two members from the Mountain, of whom Danton was one, and no

Girondins at all. Danton and Robespierre spoke of the need for winning the support of the people for the Republic. This could be done by economic concessions. On 4 May a maximum price, which the Girondins opposed, was fixed for grain and later in the month a compulsory loan was imposed on the wealthy.

All these measures – Revolutionary Tribunals, representatives-on-mission, watch committees, the Committee of Public Safety and the summary execution decree – were to become vital ingredients of the Terror. At first they were applied only partially, if at all, outside the Vendée.

b) The Overthrow of the Girondins

Danton and other Montagnards had asked the Girondins to stop attacking Parisian *sans-culottes* as *buveurs de sang* but to no avail. On 26 May Robespierre came down on the side of the *sans-culottes* when he invited 'the people to place themselves in insurrection against the corrupt [Girondin] deputies'. On 31 May a rising began which spread rapidly when news of the overthrow of the Jacobins in Lyon reached Paris on 1 June. On 2 June 80,000 National Guardsmen surrounded the Convention and directed their cannon at it. They demanded the expulsion of the Girondins from the Assembly and a maximum price on all essential goods. When the deputies tried to leave they were forced back. For the first time armed force was being used against an elected assembly. To avoid a massacre or a revolutionary commune seizing power, the Convention was compelled to agree to the arrest of 29 Girondin deputies and two ministers. Following the purge of the Girondins a young royalist, Charlotte Corday assassinated Marat in the vain belief that it would end the revolution.

c) The Federal Revolt

Following the purge of the Girondin deputies, revolts broke out in some of France's largest provincial cities. They were starting to break away from government authority. The Montagnards called these revolts 'federalism' and said that they were royalist plots to destroy the unity of the Republic, and were inspired and supported by the Girondins. In fact, both sides believed in the unity of the Republic and the revolts had, initially, nothing to do with royalism or counter-revolution. In the many departments the rebels resented the influence of Paris and its Commune over the Convention and the power of the Jacobins. The first significant city to rebel was Marseille. Its inhabitants turned against the local Jacobins club. Encouraged by these events, anti-Jacobin supporters took control of many other towns and cities in the south. The most serious revolt occurred in Lyon (30 May) – the republic's second city. Bordeaux reacted to the purge of the Girondin deputies by declaring the city in revolt until they were restored.

Some form of disturbance was taking place in 60 of the 85 departments, although there was significant resistance to the Convention in only eight. Potentially the most serious revolt was in the great naval base of Toulon. Disillusion with the war and the course of the revolution led to an uprising which overthrew the town council and closed down the Jacobin club. The government cut off food supplies to the city. To prevent starvation the town authorities negotiated with the British, who insisted that the monarchy be proclaimed. British troops entered the town on 28 August. As half the French fleet was lying off the coast at Toulon, this was a most serious blow to the republic.

Once the towns of Marseille, Lyon and Toulon had rejected the Convention, many smaller towns in the Rhône valley and Provence followed suit. How serious a threat to the government was the Federalist revolt? Despite the attempts of the Jacobin press to portray them as pro-Church monarchists, many of the federalists were supportive of the republic. Rebels in Toulon wanted '. . . to enjoy our goods, our property the fruits of our toil and industry in peace, yet we see them incessantly exposed to threats from those who have nothing themselves'.[6] However, 'Federal' forces were pitifully small. Marseille was able to raise only 3,500 men, Bordeaux 400, and none of them wanted to move far from home. This failure to co-operate enabled the government to pick off the rebel areas one by one.

Of greater concern to the government was that the war against the allies continued to go badly in the summer of 1793. The Austrians pushed into France. The Spaniards invaded Roussillon in the south. The allies had 160,000 men on the Netherlands' border with France, with a smaller French force opposing them. If York and Coburg, the allied commanders, had joined forces and moved on Paris the French would have faced disaster. Fortunately for them, the allies did not co-ordinate their plans. Pitt ordered the Duke of York to capture Dunkirk as a naval base, so he turned west. The Austrians turned east, and the allied army broke in two. This enormous blunder saved France, as did the disunity of the allies.

d) The New Committee of Public Safety

After 2 June most deputies feared and distrusted the Montagnards. However, they did not want to see the Republic overthrown by domestic or foreign enemies and so for the next 14 months they were reluctant accomplices of the Jacobin minority. When a new Committee of Public Safety was formed between July and September 1793, the 12 members were all either Montagnards, or deputies of the Plain who had joined them. All were middle class, except for Hérault de Séchelles, who was a former noble. Eight of them were lawyers, two were engineers. Nearly all were young: the average age was just 30. There was no chairman: all the members were jointly responsible for the Committee's actions.

The new Committee was to become the first strong government since the Revolution began. Barère became the spokesman of the Committee in the Convention. Carnot, an engineer, devoted his considerable energy and organising ability to the army, qualities which led Napoleon to call him 'the organiser of victory'. In September, owing to *sans-culotte* pressure, two members of the Cordeliers Club, Collot d'Herbois and Billaud-Varenne, joined the Committee. Robespierre's closest associates on the committee were Couthon, who was paralysed and confined to a wheel-chair, and Saint-Just. Proud and courageous, Saint-Just was to be a leading advocate of Terror. All the members were re-elected to the Committee by the Convention every month from September 1793 to July 1794, except for Hérault. He retired from the Committee in December 1793 and was executed with Danton in April 1794. The members of the Committee did not share the same opinions but they were prepared to forget their differences in order to deal with the pressing problems which faced France.

Maximilien Robespierre joined the Committee on 27 July. Owing to his influence in the Jacobin Club and the Commune, he was expected to provide a link between the middle-class Jacobins and the *sans-culottes*. He never had much support in the Convention and many could not stand his narrow self-righteousness. Oelsner, a German member of the Jacobin Club, wrote of him: 'I know no-one so insufferable, so arrogant, so taciturn, so boring'. Pétion, the Mayor of Paris, summed up what many thought:

> Robespierre is extremely touchy and suspicious; he sees plots, treason ... everywhere ... Imperious in his opinions, listening only to himself, intolerant of opposition, never pardoning those who had wounded his *amour-propre*, never admitting his mistakes.

Yet he was known as 'the Incorruptible' because he did not seek power or wealth for himself and was consistent in putting the good of the country above all other considerations. Some have described him as 'a moral fanatic', because his love of '*vertu*' swept aside all human feelings, as when he wrote:

> The spirit of the Republic is virtue, in other words love of one's country, that magnanimous devotion that sinks all private interests in the general interest.

To him principles were everything, human beings nothing. Anyone who did not put '*vertu*' first would have to be sacrificed:

> Terror is nothing other than justice, prompt, severe and inflexible; it is therefore an emanation of virtue ... Break the enemies of liberty with terror, and you will be justified as founders of the Republic.

His steely adherence to some principles did not prevent Robespierre from being an extremely astute politician. He usually acted with caution, waiting for the right moment and showed remarkable flair for choosing it. After Varennes he had advised against republican demonstrations, because they would give the authorities an excuse for crushing the radicals. He associated himself with the risings of 10 August 1792 and 2 June 1793 only at the last minute, when he knew they would be successful. He was to show the same skill in revolutionary government, isolating his rivals from their sympathisers before crushing them.

It was Robespierre's tactical skill which led him to ally with the *sans-culottes*. He saw the need for the Montagnards to be allied to the people if the Revolution was to survive. During the rising of 31 May–2 June he wrote in his diary:

> What is needed is one single will . . . The danger within France comes from the middle classes and to defeat them we must rally the people.

His championship of the people did not begin here but went back to the time when he was a lawyer in Arras before the Revolution. He had derived from Rousseau his belief in the sovereignty of the people and his ideal of a republic of small property-owners. He was known as the poor man's advocate when he was elected to the Estates-General in 1789, where he soon distinguished himself as a liberal and champion of the Rights of Man. He opposed the division of citizens into 'active' and 'passive' and the laws which deprived West Indian negroes of full civil rights. His economic ideas were similar to those of the *sans-culottes*. Like them, he disapproved of excessive wealth and told the Convention in April 1793 that 'the extreme disparity between rich and poor lies at the heart of many of the troubles and crimes of our society'. The common ideal of both Robespierre and the *sans-culottes* was that of small, independent producers, peasants and artisans, each owning his field or workshop. This ideal was in conflict with capitalism's belief in the concentration of industry. He did not believe in the equal distribution of property, yet he felt that the state had the obligation 'to provide for the subsistence of all its members, either by providing work for them or by providing the means of subsistence for those unable to work'.

As Robespierre shared many ideas with the *sans-culottes* he was popular with the people of Paris but he was never one of them. He dressed with the silk stockings, knee-breeches and powdered wig of the old regime. He never took part in a demonstration and was never carried shoulder-high by the people, as Marat was. Robespierre was a rather remote figure who lived comfortably, though not ostentatiously, in the *petit-bourgeois* household of the cabinet maker Duplay.

References

1   Alfred Cobban, *A History of Modern France Vol 1* (London. 1957) p. 210. A more recent study casts doubt on the significance of the content of the

armoire der fer while acknowledging its great propaganda value. See Richard Cobb and Colin Jones (ed) *The French Revolution. Voices from a momentous epoch 1789–1795* (London, 1988) p. 169.

2 D.M.G. Sutherland, *France 1789–1815: Revolution and Counter-Revolution* (Fontana,1985) p. 166.

3 John Hardman, *Louis XVI and the French Revolution* (History Review, September 1996) p. 41.

4 James Roberts, *The Counter-Revolution in France 1787–1830* (Macmillan, 1990) p. 23.

5 Quoted in Cobb and Jones, *op cit.* p. 176.

6 Quoted in William Doyle, *op cit.* p. 240.

Working on Chapter 4

This chapter relates to the growing radicalisation of the revolution and the deep tensions between the Jacobins and the Girondins. These divisions contributed to several uprisings in the provinces. The course of the war was also posing problems. These two crises threatened the very survival of the republic, and the response of the Jacobins was a highly centralised dictatorship through the Committee of Public Safety. Write notes to explain how the crisis led to a dictatorship and to describe what policies were passed to try to preserve the revolution. To strengthen your understanding of how the Jacobin government responded to the crisis, draw up a table with three columns. In one column give details of each measure/decree which was passed. In the second column explain how it was designed to deal with the crisis. In the third column evaluate its success.

Answering essay and structured questions on Chapter 4

It is important that when you are presented with an essay question, you recognise the type of question which is set. There are three main types of question that you are most likely to come across. These are – analytical, evaluative or judgemental questions. A question which starts with 'Why', will expect you to set out reasons, in order of importance bearing in mind how complex it is to explain historical events. The use of phrases and words such as – 'To what extent', 'How far', 'Assess', 'Discuss' or 'Comment' will require you to analyse and evaluate and reach a decision or judgement, based on your argument. If a quotation is provided it implies that there is a view for you to discuss. You can accept or reject the view as you wish. Answers which attain a higher level of marks will often end up challenging or modifying the view in the quotation rather than just accepting it at face value. Essay questions relating to this chapter are most likely to deal with the outbreak of the war. These will usually focus on why the war started, or what the consequences of the way the conflict evolved were. Consider the following two examples:

I Why was most of Europe at war with Revolutionary France by the end of 1793?

In answering this question you will need to discuss fully the various reasons for the war beginning in 1792. Various groups had their own reasons for urging war, and these will need to be fully considered. Brissot and the Girondin hoped to use the war to spread revolutionary ideas and to consolidate the revolution. It is important that you consider the motivation of Louis, the émigrés and the other European royal families. They hoped that a disastrous war might speed up the restoration of Louis' former powers and prevent the spread of revolution. Refer back to your notes. In your plan write down the various reasons and then try and arrange them in order of importance.

2 To what extent did the war bring about a change in the course of the Revolution?

This is a more difficult question than the previous one in that it requires a degree of evaluation. You will need to consider whether the war changed the direction of the revolution and if so how. Republicanism emerged before the war but gathered momentum during it. The war crisis in 1793 certainly contributed to the emergence of a strong centralised government. Did it contribute to the triumph of the Jacobin? Consider also whether the revolts were in any way brought about by the war or general antipathy to Paris. A factor in the Vendée rebellion was the opposition to conscription and the authority of the central government. An effective response to this question will require you to engage in an argument and to reach a judgement.

The following are two examples of structured questions relating to this chapter. The format with a structured question will usually involve two parts. The first part will as a rule require you to describe or explain why something occurred – it will test your factual recall. As long as your answer is accurate and relevant then you should score quite well on the first part. In the second part you will be asked to evaluate the factors behind an event. You will need to be selective in material which you use. The question will very likely involve a number of issues and you may need to come to some sort of a judgement. Consider the following examples:

I **(a)** Describe the main features of the political struggle between the Girondins and Jacobins. (*15 marks*)

(b) Why did revolts break out in France during the spring and summer of 1793? (*15 marks*)

2 **(a)** Explain why the monarchy was abolished and Louis XVI executed in 1793. (*15 marks*)

(b) How well did the Jacobin government succeed in dealing with the crisis confronting it in 1792–3? (*15 marks*)

5 Government by Terror 1793–4

POINTS TO CONSIDER

You are now considering the most dramatic and famous phase of the revolution – the Terror. For many this phase was symbolic of the chaos and anarchy into which events in France had degenerated. You will need to consider what policies the new government adopted and decide whether or not they were successful. This phase is very clearly linked to the war, the desire to preserve the republic from its various enemies, and the figure of Robespierre. Were all the sacrifices, many in the shadow of the guillotine, ultimately worth it? As you read, pay close attention to the emergence of political extremism, the struggle for power and the role of the *sans-culottes*.

KEY DATES

1793	**Apr**	Committee of Public Safety created (6th)
	Jun	Girondin deputies purged (2nd), Constitution of 1793 accepted (24th)
	Jul	Robespierre joined the CPS
	Aug	Decree of levée en masse issued
	Sept	Government by Terror, Law of Suspects (17th), Year II began (22nd), Maximum introduced (29th)
	Dec	Vendean rebels defeated (23rd)
1794	**Mar**	Hébertists executed (24th)
	Apr	Danton and Desmoulins executed (5th)
	Jun	Festival of the Supreme Being (8th)
	Jul	Coup of Thermidor – Robespierre overthrown (27th–28th)

The symbol of the Terror is the guillotine and it is this image which most people have in mind when they think of the French Revolution. Bloodthirsty purges, terrified citizens, dictatorship and the suppression of the liberties which had been so triumphantly announced in the Declaration of Rights of 1789: all are associated with the Terror. While the terror is the most dramatic phase of the revolution it had less influence on the formation of modern France than the great reforms of the Constituent Assembly (see pages 40–48 above). The French historians Furet and Richet saw the period from August 1792 to July 1794 as a time when extremist *sans-culottes* knocked the Revolution off-course.[1] They forced the country's leaders to adopt policies which were contrary to the liberal reforms of the Constituent Assembly. Their support was necessary to preserve the Revolution but they did not make any permanent gains for themselves or any lasting changes. After the fall of Robespierre, the Revolution, they maintain, returned to its earlier course.

Why did government by terror emerge? According to Richard Cobb 'It came into being because of the need to organise the country against the possibility of treason and military defeat.'[2] There were two periods of Terror and both are associated with the war abroad. The first began with the attack on the Tuileries on 10 August 1792, included the September Massacres and came to an end with the battle of Valmy, when the allied invasion was held up and then pushed back. The second period began with the *journée* of 31 May–2 June 1793, when some Girondin deputies were arrested, and ended with the execution of Robespierre and his supporters in July 1794. This second Terror began when French armies were doing badly and France was once again faced with invasion. Its end came shortly after the victory of Fleurus in June 1794, which made the French frontiers secure.

1 The Dominance of the *Sans-culottes*

> **KEY ISSUES** Who were the *sans-culottes*? What did they hope to achieve?

The growth in power of the *sans-culottes* was largely a consequence of the war. They had played an important role in the Revolution in 1789 by storming the Bastille and in bringing the King to Paris in the October Days, but after that the bourgeois National Guard was used to keep them under control, as it did at the Champ de Mars. The first opportunity for *sans-culotte* militants came with the opening of the National Guard to 'passive' citizens in July 1792. They were important in the overthrow of the monarchy and from the summer of 1792 to the spring of 1794 no one could control Paris without obtaining their support. They were responsible for the *journée* of 31 May–2 June 1793 which brought the Jacobins to power.

a) Their Ideas and Organisation

Who were the *sans-culottes*? Their own view of themselves is illuminating: 'A *sans-culotte*? He's a man who goes everywhere on foot, who has none of the millions you're all after, no mansions, no servants and who lives simply on the fourth or fifth floor. In the evening he's at his section to support sound resolutions. A *sans-culotte* always keeps his sword sharp. At the first roll of the drum off he goes to the Vendée or the *armée du Nord*.'[3] They hated the aristocracy and anyone of great wealth, and had a fierce devotion to equality. They addressed everyone as citizen. Their red caps, originally associated with freed slaves, symbolised the equality of all citizens. They were passionately anticlerical because priests had joined with aristocrats in taking the wealth created by ordinary men and women. Along with their desire for equality went a belief in direct democracy. For the *sans-culottes* the sovereignty of the people could not be delegated to representatives. The people had the right to control and change their elected representative at any time and if they were betrayed they had the right of insurrection. Political life must take place in the open: the patriot had no reason to hide his opinions. The meetings of the Assembly must therefore be open to the public and deputies must vote aloud.

The majority of *sans-culottes* were wage-earners but they were not the ones who held power in the Sections. Each Section was controlled by a small minority of militants, who were usually the better-off members, because they had the time to devote to Section business. Of the 454 members of the Revolutionary Committees in Paris in 1793–4, 65 per cent were shopkeepers, small workshop masters and independent craftsmen; 26 per cent were rentiers, civil servants and members of the liberal professions; only eight per cent were wage-earners. They exercised power through their own institutions, which were not responsible to the central government. The Commune and the Sections were the administrative units of Parisian local government, with their officials and elected committees. They had their own police and armed forces, as they controlled the National Guard. They also controlled the popular societies. These were encouraged by the government as long as there was danger from internal and foreign foes, as they helped the war effort, kept a watch on suspects and assisted representatives-on-mission in purging local authorities. In 1793 they were often more important than the municipalities, as they issued 'certificates of citizenship', without which no-one could be employed.

The Parisian *sans-culottes* had the force with which to seize power but they chose to persuade or intimidate the Convention, never to replace it. They wholeheartedly supported the government on basic issues, such as in their hatred of the aristocracy and in their determination to win the war.

b) Concessions to the Sans-culottes

The *sans-culottes* had put the Jacobins in power, so a new Constitution, which recognised many of their aspirations, was rushed through the Assembly in June 1793. It was preceded by a Declaration of Rights, which went much further than that of 1789, as it stated the rights of people to work, to have assistance in time of need and to be educated. The right of insurrection, one of the *sans-culottes'* most cherished beliefs, was proclaimed. All adult males were to have the vote and there were to be direct elections.

More soldiers were needed to fight the war, so the Sections also demanded conscription. This came with the *levée en masse* on 23 August 1793. It marked the appearance of total war. 'Until the enemies of France have been expelled from the territory of the Republic, all Frenchmen are in a state of permanent requisition for the army'.[4] The task for the Committee of Public Safety was enormous. The first group of conscripts, unmarried men between 18 and 25, numbered nearly half a million. They had to be fed, armed and trained, so all the human and material resources of the nation were put at the government's disposal. State factories were set up to make arms and ammunition. Church bells were melted down for cannon and religious vessels for coinage. The government also took over the control of foreign trade and shipping. The resources for economic planning did not really exist, yet the controlled economy harnessed the energies of the nation on an unprecedented scale. It was remarkably successful in the short-term: without it victory would have been impossible.

The *sans-culottes* hoped in the first instance to preserve the republic. To achieve this they actively supported measures which challenged privilege and inequality. They were active in helping to suppress the counter revolution, and ensure that Paris was well supplied with provisions and adequately defended.

2 The Impact of the Terror

> **KEY ISSUE** What policies were introduced by the government to preserve the republic?

a) The *Journée* of 4–5 September 1793

The economic situation continued to deteriorate in the summer. In mid-August the assignat was below a third of its face value and drought reduced the grain imports into Paris by three-quarters. One group, the *Enragés*, and their spokesman Jacques Roux demanded action. As a priest, in one of the poorest quarters of Paris, Roux was shocked by what he saw: people starving in crowded attics. These were people for whom the Revolution had done nothing. His followers were wage-earners, casual labourers, the poor and unemployed. He wanted the Convention to do something about starvation and poverty and when it did nothing, he denounced it. His programme was economic Terror, the execution of hoarders who pushed up the price of grain and a purge of ex-nobles from the army.[5] Robespierre wanted to destroy him, because he was threatening the Commune and the Convention with direct action in the streets. Roux was arrested, and died in prison in February 1794.

On 4 September a crowd gathered before the Hôtel de Ville to demand bread and higher wages and on 5 September it marched on the Convention, forcing it to accept a series of radical measures. The Sections imposed on the Convention the proclamation of 'Terror as the order of the day'.

One instrument of the Terror the Convention immediately authorised was the formation of a Parisian '*armée révolutionnaire*'. A proposal to raise a people's army had been agreed in June but attempts to carry out the plan had been frustrated until September. 'The *armées révolutionnaires* were born out of fear'.[6] Fear of counter revolution. Robespiere envisaged a *sans-culotte* army which could energise the defence of the republic. Subsequently, 56 other armies, unauthorised, were set up in the provinces between September and December 1793, and were used in about two-thirds of the departments. These civilian armies were to ensure the food supplies of Paris and the large provincial cities, and round up deserters from the army, hoarders, refractory priests, religious 'fanatics', political suspects and royalist rebels. The armies were also to mobilise the nation's resources for the war effort by confiscating church silver and bells. They were to establish revolutionary 'justice' in the areas of the south and west, which had shown little enthusiasm for the Revolution.

There were about 6,000 in the Parisian *armée révolutionnaire* plus 1,200 artillery men, and 30,000 in the provincial armies. Very few were wage-earners: the majority were *sans-culotte* militants – shopkeepers and craftsmen. The operation of the Parisian army extended over 25 departments. Its main task was to ensure the capital's food supplies by requisitions in the great grain-producing areas of the north. A third of its men took part in the savage repression of the federal revolt at Lyon. Both the Parisian and provincial armies were engaged in dechristianisation (see page 86). The Parisian army was remarkably successful in supplying Paris with bread until the spring of 1794, and so helped to preserve the Revolution. The provincial armies also did a good job in supplying major towns and the line army on the eastern frontier. Their success, however, was likely to be short-term, partly because their numbers were small and partly because of the unremitting hostility of the rural population to their work. Yet the joy shown in the countryside when they were disbanded was an indication of just how successful they had been.

The Committee of Public Safety did not like the revolutionary armies because they were anarchic and outside the control of the authorities. They also disliked them because they created opposition to the Revolution by their heavy-handed methods in dealing with the peasants. Robespierre, who had supported the armies up to September 1793, turned against them because of their 'dechristianisation' campaign. (See page 86.) The Convention had accepted the Parisian army only with great reluctance and never recognised its counterparts raised in the provinces. They were doomed once the revolutionary government was firmly established.

b) Economic Terror

The Convention had bowed to popular pressure from Roux and the *sans-culottes* in July by passing a law which made death the penalty for hoarding food and other supplies. This probably did more harm than good. Shortages were made worse as merchants refused to carry large stocks, in case they were accused of hoarding. The Convention introduced price control when it passed the law of the General Maximum on 29 September. The new law fixed the price not only of bread but of many essential goods and services at one third above the prices of June 1790. There was no point in fixing prices unless wages were also controlled, as they largely determined what prices would be. Wages were fixed at 50 per cent above the level of 1790. When peasants refused to sell grain at the maximum price, requisitioning (compulsory sale to the government) was allowed as the only way to feed the towns and the armies.

The Maximum divided the common people against each other. The peasants hated it because it was often below the cost of production, so they avoided it whenever possible. The *sans-culottes* wanted it so that they could afford to live. When they went into the countryside with the *armée révolutionnaire* to enforce the Maximum they clashed with the peasants and the conflict between town and country was exacerbated. The government was in a difficult position, as farmers would simply stop sowing if they could not make a profit. The co-operation of the wealthy peasants, who controlled most of the harvest, was necessary for the government. They were the municipal councillors and tax collectors, who were expected to oversee requisitioning. Thus the Maximum had to be carried out, where there was no local revolutionary army, by the rich in the countryside. To try to meet their concerns the government revised prices upwards in February 1794, much to the disgust of the *sans-culottes*.

The government's measures were successful in the short-term. The towns and armies were fed and the assignat, worth 22 per cent of its face value in August, rose to 48 per cent in December 1793.

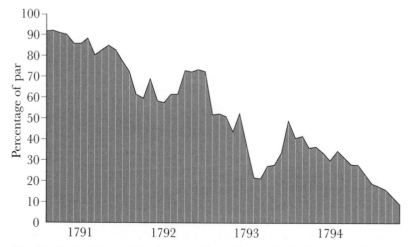

The Declining Value of the *Assignat* (from *The French Revolution: An Economic Interpretation* by F. Aftalion, Cambridge University Press, 1990)

c) The Political Terror

The Political Terror took three forms. There was the official Terror, controlled by the Committees of Public Safety and of General Security, which was centered in Paris and whose victims came before the Revolutionary Tribunal. There was the Terror in the areas of federal revolt, where the worst atrocities took place. There was also the Terror in other parts of France, under the control of watch committees, representatives-on-mission and the revolutionary armies.

The Committees, mainly the Committee of General Security, were responsible for bringing cases before the Revolutionary Tribunal in Paris. Up to September 1793 the Tribunal had heard 260 cases and pronounced 66 death sentences (26 per cent of the total). For Robespierre and the Montagnards, Terror had to be legal and controlled by the government. In staging a series of celebrity trials they were giving way to popular demands but also getting rid of people they genuinely regarded as enemies of the Republic. What mattered was the decision to prosecute, as the verdict was automatic – death. Acquittal would have been regarded as a vote of no confidence in the government. The Revolutionary Tribunal became the scene of endless trials and death sentences: Marie Antoinette on 16 October, 31 Girondin deputies on 31 October, Philippe Égalité on 6 November and Mme Roland, wife of the Girondin ex-minister, three days later.

By the end of 1793 the federal revolt had been put down by the regular army. Marseille, Lyon and Toulon were taken and the Vendéan rebels were crushed. Repression followed. General Westermann told the Committee of Public Safety: 'The Vendée is no more . . . It has died beneath our sabres, together with its women and children . . . I have crushed the children under my horses' hooves, massacred the women – they, at least, will not give birth to any more brigands.' From January to May 1794 troops moved through the area, shooting almost every peasant they met, burning farms and crops and killing their animals. Women were raped and mutilated. When the 'pacification' was over, the Vendée was a depopulated desert. Thousands who surrendered crammed the prisons. They could not be released in case they joined the rebels again, so they too were shot without trial – 2,000 near Angers alone. In the Vendée 7,000 were condemned by revolutionary courts, half the total for the whole of France. Most of these were peasants; few were bourgeois.

Representatives-on-mission were often responsible for the worst atrocities. Their actions were fully supported and indeed were encouraged by the government. Hérault de Séchelles, a member of the Committee of Public Safety, told Carrier 'You must be ruthless in purging and imprisoning every single suspect. Liberty has not yet been achieved. We can afford to be humane only when we are sure of victory.'[7] At Nantes, Carrier carried out the dreadful '*noyades*' (drownings). About 1,800 people, nearly half of them women, were put in barges, which were taken to the mouth of the Loire and sunk. In Toulon 800 were shot without trial and a further 282 were sent to the guillotine by a Revolutionary Commission. Lyon was the second city in France and was to pay dearly for its rebellion. Couthon had directed the siege at Lyon and felt that only moderate repression was needed. However, Robespierre wanted 'inexorable severity', as humane measures would simply encourage new conspiracies. The Committee of Public Safety ordered (12 October 1793) that 'The name of Lyon shall be wiped off the list of towns of the Republic. There shall be built a monument above the ruins – 'Lyons made war on liberty. Lyon no longer exists'. Couthon was replaced by Collot and Fouché, aided by a detachment of the Parisian revolutionary army. During the *mitraillade* victims were mown down by cannon fire in front of large pits, and many others were guillotined, about 1900 in all. It was in these rebel areas of the west and south-east, which covered only five departments, that 70 per cent of total executions during the Terror took place. Even here, they were confined to limited areas: there were hundreds of executions at Nantes but hardly a dozen at nearby Rouen.

The Terror was carried to other parts of France by representatives-on-mission and revolutionary armies. The representatives were fanatical Jacobins, who packed the new revolutionary committees with their supporters. The government had delegated its powers, under the Law of Suspects of September 1793, to these committees. They could arrest anyone they thought was a danger to the Republic and imprison them indefinitely without trial. A mass arrest of suspects took place (about half a million according to one estimate, of whom 10,000 died in prison). The committees could also send offenders before one of the Revolutionary Tribunals, and purge the local administration, removing moderates and replacing them by *sans-culottes* militants. These committees symbolised the Terror at the local level. By the end of 1793 most rural communes had one. They were the one permanent institution of the Terror in the countryside.

In many rural areas there was little enthusiasm for the Republic. Saint-André, a member of the Committee of Public Safety, reported from Lot that grass-roots democracy had produced communes which were indifferent or hostile to the Revolution. Support for it would have disappeared completely in most parts of France without representatives, clubs and watch committees. Even so, local Jacobins often did not enjoy much support. At Estaing (Aveyron) they could raise only two dozen supporters out of a population of 900.

What was the human cost of the terror? Figures relating to deaths during this period vary enormously, from several hundred thousand at the top end of the range to tens of thousands at the lower end. One reason for the variation is that different ways of counting the figures were used. Sometimes official figures were used and sometimes estimates were made of deaths from all causes – starvation, military action, prison deaths etc. One study of the Terror has estimated that there were 17,000 official executions, 16 per cent of them in Paris and most of the rest in areas of revolt (52 per cent in the Vendée and 19 per cent in the south-east).[8] Of the victims 28 per cent were peasants, mainly from the Vendée and 31 per cent were urban workers, especially from Lyon and Marseille. It is clear that the majority of the victims of the terror perished in the Vendée. Douglas Johnson suggests a figure of 80,000 deaths for the Vendée, and for the whole of the west a round figure of 200,000 would seem to be realistic.[9]

d) Dechristianisation

Dechristianisation was not an invention of the central government. It began in the provinces and the Convention was drawn along with it.[10] What was dechristianisation? It was a deliberate attempt by the first republic between 1792 and 1794 to use the resources of the state to destroy Christianity as the dominant cultural form of French society. In its place would be created system linked more closely to the revolution.[11] The attack on the Church took various forms. Churches were closed, church bells and silver were removed, roadside shrines and crosses were destroyed, and priests were sometimes forced to marry. There were few non-juring priests left in France by late 1793, so the dechristianisation movement became an attack on the constitutional Church, which had failed to persuade the peasants to support the Revolution. Many constitutional clergy supported the Lyon rising, so dechristianisation became part of the struggle against counter-revolution. Although the Convention was unsympathetic to Catholicism and to priests, it only connived at the attack on the Church. It did not encourage it.

In October a new revolutionary calendar was introduced to replace the Christian calendar. The new calendar was dated from 22 September 1792, when the Republic was proclaimed. Thus the period from 22 September 1792 to 21 September 1793 became Year 1. The year was divided into twelve months of 30 days, with five supplementary days (soon called *sans-culottides*). Each month was divided into three periods of ten days, every tenth day (*decadi*) being a day of rest. Another decree gave each month a name appropriate to its season: thus Vendémiaire (the month of vintage) ran from 22 September to 21 October, Floréal (the month of flowers) from 20 April to 19 May. The new calendar ignored Sundays and festivals of the Church.

The main impulse for the dechristianisation campaign came from the *sans-culottes* in the Paris Commune, the revolutionary armies and from the representatives-on-mission. They hated Catholicism, which they felt had betrayed the Revolution. Like the abolition of the monarchy, the destruction of churches was a symbol of their determination to destroy everything connected with the old regime. The Paris Commune stopped paying clerical salaries in May 1793 and in

November ordered that all churches in Paris should be closed. Notre Dame became a Temple of Reason. This movement spread rapidly throughout France. By the spring of 1794 most churches in France had been closed. The most enthusiastic dechristianisers were representatives like Fouché, who placed signs above the entrance to cemeteries which read, 'Death is an eternal sleep'.

Priests were forced to renounce their priesthood and many were compelled to marry. Estimates of the number of priests who gave up their calling vary from about 6,000 (ten per cent of all constitutional priests) to 20,000. This brutal attempt to uproot centuries of Christian belief was deeply resented in the villages. For many ordinary people outside the civil war zones and the main communication routes, dechristianisation, which left large areas of France without priests, was the aspect of the Terror which most affected them.

3 The Dictatorship of the Committee of Public Safety

> **KEY ISSUES** What did the Committee of Public Safety achieve? Why was Robespierre overthrown during Thermidor?

Towards the end of 1793 the government was overcoming the problems which had threatened the existence of the Republic. The federal revolts had been crushed, the towns were being fed and the *assignat* was rising in value. In the west, defeats of the rebels at Cholet and Le Mans effectively ended the civil war in the Vendée. French armies were also doing well in the war. By the end of September they had driven the Spanish armies out of Roussillon and the Piedmontese out of Savoy. The British were defeated at Hondschoote in the same month and the Austrians at Wattignies in October. It appeared that the Committee of Public Safety's policy for defending France was proving to be successful. With renewed confidence the Convention's Committees could now begin to claw back much of the power which had passed to the *sans-culottes* and their organisations.

A conflict between the government and the *sans-culottes* was inevitable at some stage. There was administrative anarchy in the departments in the autumn of 1793 as local revolutionary committees, revolutionary armies and representatives such as Fouché interpreted the law, or ignored it, just as they pleased. No government could tolerate anarchy indefinitely, yet it had to act carefully.

The first steps to tame the popular movement were taken in September 1793. The Convention decided that the general assemblies of the Sections could meet only twice a week. In October the Convention passed a decree that government was to be 'revolutionary until the peace'. This meant the indefinite suspension of the Constitution of 1793. It was never put into operation.

a) The Law of 4 December (14 Frimaire) 1793

A major step to central control came with the law of 4 December which established Revolutionary Government. The two Committees, whilst deriving their authority solely from the Convention, were given full executive powers. The Committee of General Security was responsible for police and internal security: thus the Revolutionary Tribunal, as well as the surveillance committees, came under its control. The Committee of Public Safety had more extensive powers. In addition to controlling ministers and generals, it was to control foreign policy and purge and direct local government. The chief officials of the communes and departments, who had been elected, were placed under 'national agents' appointed by and responsible to the central government. The representatives-on-mission, sent out by the Convention in April, were now put firmly under the control of the Committee of Public Safety. All revolutionary armies, except that in Paris, were to be disbanded.

Robespierre's speech on the Principles of Revolutionary Government. 25 December 1793

'The theory of revolutionary government is as new as the revolution which has developed it . . . the function of government is to direct the moral and physical resources of the nation towards its essential aim. The aim of constitutional government is to preserve the Republic; that of revolutionary government is to put the republic on a secure foundation. The revolution is the war of liberty against its enemies: the constitution is the regime of victorious and peace-loving liberty. Revolutionary government needs to be extraordinarily active, precisely because it is at war. It is subject to less uniform and rigorous rules, because the circumstances in which it finds itself are tempestuous and changing, and above all because it is obliged to employ ceaselessly new and urgent resources for new and pressing threats.Constitutional government is primarily concerned with civil liberty: revolutionary government with public liberty. Under a constitutional regime it is more or less enough to protect individuals against abuses of government. Under a revolutionary regime the government itself is obliged to defend itself against all the factions which threaten it. Revolutionary government gives public protection to good citizens; to the enemies of the people it deals out only death . . . If revolutionary government has to be more active in its policies and more free in its actions than ordinary government, is it just less legitimate? No; it rests on the most sacred of all laws – the safety of the people; and on the most irrefutable of all arguments – that of necessity. Revolutionary government has rules of its own, resting on the principles of justice and public

> order. It has no room for anarchy and disorder. It is not directed
> by individual feelings, but by the public interest. It is necessary to
> navigate between two rocks; weakness and boldness, reaction and
> extremism.'

This marked the end of anarchy and reduced the power of the *sans-culottes*. It gave France her first strong government since 1787. It also marked a complete reversal of the principles of 1789. The Constitutions of 1791 and 1793 had established decentralisation, elections to all posts, the separation of legislative from executive power and non-political justice. Now all this was changed and many of the characteristics of the *ancien régime* reappeared. Robespierre justified this by saying that a dictatorship was necessary until foreign and internal enemies of the Revolution were destroyed. 'We must', he said, 'organise the despotism of liberty to crush the despotism of kings'. It was contrary to the ideas of democracy and people's rights he had advocated when he had been out of office.

b) Opposition to the Government – Hébert and Danton

The main challenge to the revolutionary government came from within the ranks of former supporters. 'Left' opposition came from Hébert and his followers. His newspaper *Le Père Duchesne*, demanded that more hoarders should be executed and that there should be a redistribution of property. It was very popular with the *sans-culottes*. The Hébertistes had few supporters in the Convention but many in the Cordeliers Club, the Commune, the Paris revolutionary army and the popular societies. Robespierre disliked their political extremism, particularly their leading part in the dechristianisation campaign, which turned Catholics against the Revolution.

At the beginning of March Hébert announced in the Cordeliers Club that an insurrection was necessary 'that shall bring death to those who oppress us'. It is possible that Hébert was not attempting to seize power but simply wanted a mass demonstration to put pressure on the government. Whatever he wanted, he was not acting in response to popular pressure and there was little response from the Sections. Robespierre decided the time had come to destroy him. Hébert and 18 supporters were arrested. They were accused of being foreign agents who wanted a military dictatorship which would prepare the way for a restored monarchy. The populace was taken in by this government propaganda. When the Hébertistes were guillotined on 24 March, Paris remained calm.

The Committee took advantage of the situation to strengthen its dictatorship. The Parisian revolutionary army was disbanded, the Cordeliers Club was closed and popular societies were forced to disband. The Commune was purged and filled with supporters of Robespierre. Representatives-on-mission, responsible for some of the worst atrocities in the provinces, were recalled to Paris.

Of greater significance, because of the higher profile of its leader, was the opposition of the right. This centred around Danton, a former colleague of Robespierre, and leading Jacobin. The Indulgents, as they were known, wanted to halt the terror and the centralisation imposed in December. In order to heal the divisions in the revolutionary movement, Danton argued that the war would have to come to an end, as it was largely responsible for the Terror. Since leaving office he had become very wealthy. It was not clear where his new-found wealth came from. Nearly 400,000 livres spent by the Ministry of Justice when he was in charge could not be accounted for. It appeared that Danton was corrupt. He was accused of being bribed by foreign powers, a damaging accusation which had also been levelled at Hébert.

Danton's friend, Camille Desmoulins, supported him in his desire to end the Terror. Desmoulins had asked in his newspaper, *Le Vieux Cordelier*, as early as December 1793 for the release of '200,000 citizens who are called suspects'. The publisher Nicolas Ruault commented on the situation as it was developing:

1　It is sad to see the patriots destroying each other and thus weakening both their own strength and their cause. Some who have long preached murder and death, who made 'Terror the order of the day', such as Danton and Camille Desmoulins, now feel this so strongly that they are
5　retracing their steps and suggesting 'clemency committees' instead of the revolutionary committees.

The Committee of Public Safety regarded Danton as a threat because, unlike Hébert, he had a large following in the Convention. His policies of peace and an end to the Terror would, they felt, leave the door open for a return of the monarchy. He was, therefore, brought before the Revolutionary Tribunal and on 5 April 1794 was executed with many of his followers, including Desmoulins. The Terror now seemed to have a momentum of its own. The members of the Committees had become brutalised and acted vindictively in ways of which they would have been ashamed only two years earlier. Desmoulins' wife tried to organise a demonstration in his support. She was arrested and in April went to the scaffold, along with the wife of Hébert. In no way could they be regarded as presenting a threat to the Committee.

The effect of the fall of Hébert and Danton was to stifle all criticism of the Committee of Public Safety. Everyone lived in an atmosphere of hatred and suspicion, in which deputies were afraid to say anything, because an unguarded word could lead to a death sentence. Thibaudeau, a Montagnard deputy, described the situation in his memoirs:

GEORGE JACQUES DANTON (1759–1794)

1759 born in Arcis-sur-Aube, son of a lawyer
1780 goes to Paris
1785 called to the Bar
1789 involved in politics, becomes President of the Cordeliers Club
1791 Administrator of the *Départment* of Paris. Assistant Procureur of the Commune
1792 Appointed Minister of Justice Elected deputy to the Convention; 1st Mission to Belgium
1793 2nd Mission to Belgium. Member of CPS. Retires to country because of ill health. Returns to Paris in November urges the slowing down of the Terror
1794 executed, April 5

Danton was one of the most controversial figures of the Revolution. He was loathed and loved in almost equal measure. Many hated him because he was suspected of being corrupt, untrustworthy and in the pay of the royal family. Others loved him for his vast energy, determination and fine oratory. As Minister of Justice he delivered a rousing speech calling for the defence of the nation, after the fall of Verdun to the Prussians (September 1792).

'Now is the moment for the National Assembly to become a true council of war. We ask that anyone who refuses to serve in person or to take up arms should be punished by death.

'We ask that an organising body be set up to coordinate citizens movements and we ask that messengers be sent to all the departments to notify them of the decrees which you have issued.

'The tocsin that we are going to sound is no alarm bell, it is the signal for the charge against the enemies of the fatherland. To vanquish them we must show daring, more daring, and again daring; and France will be saved'.

Following his removal from the CPS he began to criticise the policy of Terror. He was labelled an Indulgent. Fears that he might emerge as a leader of the opposition led to his arrest. After a rigged trial he was executed.

1   The National Convention was itself no more than a nominal parliament, a passive instrument of the Terror. From the ruins of its independence arose that monstrous dictatorship which grew to such fame under the name of Committee of Public Safety. The Terror isolated and stupefied
5   the deputies just as it did ordinary citizens. On entering the Assembly each member, full of distrust, watched his words and actions lest a crime be made out of them. And indeed everything mattered: where you sat, a gesture, a look, a murmur or a smile.

c) The Great Terror

The government wanted to be in complete control of repression, so in May 1794 it abolished all the provincial Revolutionary Tribunals. All enemies of the Republic had now to be brought to Paris, to be tried by the Revolutionary Tribunal there. This did not mean that the Terror would become less severe. Though the 'factions' of Danton and Hébert had been crushed, some of their supporters were still alive, so the Terror would have to continue until they were eliminated. Robespierre was unconcerned with protecting the innocent, if this let dangerous enemies of the Revolution escape.

After attempts had been made to murder them both, Robespierre and Couthon drafted the Law of Prairial, which was passed on 10 June 1794. 'Enemies of the people' were defined as 'those who have sought to mislead opinion . . . to deprave customs and to corrupt the public conscience'. These terms were so vague that almost anyone could be included. No witnesses were to be called and judgment was to be decided by 'the conscience of the jurors' rather than by any evidence produced. Defendants were not allowed defence counsel and the only verdicts possible were death or acquittal. This law removed any semblance of a fair trial and was designed to speed up the process of revolutionary justice. In this it succeeded. More people were sentenced to death in Paris, by the Revolutionary Tribunal during June/July 1794 (1594, 59.3 per cent) than in the previous 14 months of its existence. Many of the victims were nobles and clergymen, while nearly a half were members of the wealthier bourgeoisie.

The President of the Tribunal wrote to the Committee of Public Safety: 'Perhaps we should purge the prisons at a simple stroke and rid the soil of liberty of this refuse.' The Committee's response, 'Approved', was signed by Robespierre, Barère and Billaud, though Barère later tried to put all the blame on Robespierre, commenting:

> Every mind was paralysed by the ascendancy Robespierre had won over the Jacobins and bent beneath the cruel yoke of the terror he had organised. The law was passed by the silence of the legislators rather than by their agreement.

No-one dared to make any criticism of the Committee. 'The Revolution is frozen', Saint-Just commented. There were however doubts regarding the policy. Ruault expressed the general revulsion at the Great Terror, when he wrote:

1 In recent weeks we have seen the deaths of all the greatest and most famous still surviving in France and the richest too . . . all the rest of the Lamoignon family and almost the whole of the *Parlement* of Paris; the famous Lavoisier and almost all his colleagues, the Farmers-General,
5 former members of the Constituent Assembly, such as Le Chapelier, as well as Mme Elisabeth, sister of Louis XVI, etc.
   Who will ever believe that Lavoisier and the others were supporters of slavery or tyranny? No, but they were noble, rich and enlightened; they had to be put to death. The Committee of Public Safety are
10 nothing but . . . *sans-culotte* chieftains. This winter and spring the Committee has done marvels for the good of the state and the defence of the fatherland. It has produced fourteen armies out of nowhere, saltpeter, guns and cannon by the thousand, by the million. But now it is making itself detested by the horror and frequency of executions, which
15 are quite unnecessary. Whatever sort of government may be in power, it has and always will have its critics, people who dislike it. Is that a reason for killing them?

d) Robespierre Loses Support

Robespierre believed in God and had a genuine faith in life after death, in which the virtuous would be rewarded. He loathed the dechristianisation campaign of the *sans-culottes*, partly on religious grounds and partly because it upset Catholics and created enemies of the Revolution. He wanted to unite all Frenchmen in a new religion, the Cult of the Supreme Being, which he persuaded the Convention to accept in a decree of 7 May 1794. It began: 'The people of France recognises the existence of the Supreme Being and of immortality of the soul'. This new religion pleased no-one. Catholics were distressed because it ignored Catholic doctrine, liturgy and the Pope. Anti-clericals, including most members of the Committee of General Security, opposed it because they thought it was the first cautious step to reintroduce Roman Catholicism. They felt that Robespierre was setting himself up as the high priest of the new religion.

Robespierre was also losing the support of the popular movement. The *sans-culottes* had become disillusioned by the execution of the Hébertistes, by the dissolution of their popular societies and by the end of direct democracy in the Sections. They were aggrieved also by the raising of the Maximum on prices in March. This led to inflation and by July the *assignat* had fallen to 36 per cent of its face value. When the Commune was under the control of the Hébertistes it had not applied the Maximum on wages, which had risen considerably above the limit allowed. The government decided it would have to act, as the profits of manufacturers were disappearing. On 23 July, therefore, the Commune, now staffed by Robespierre's supporters, decided to apply the Maximum to wages. This led to a fall in wages by as much as a half, and heightened discontent amongst the majority of *sans-culottes*, who were wage-earners, although the employers amongst the *sans-culottes* welcomed it.

The Great Terror sickened the population, workers as well as bourgeoisie. After victory in the foreign war and the defeat of the Republic's internal enemies, it no longer seemed necessary. French armies had taken the offensive in the spring of 1794 and, after defeating the Austrians at Fleurus on 26 June, they recaptured Belgium. All foreign troops were driven from France, and French armies moved into the Rhineland and crossed the Alps and the Pyrenees.

Yet the dictatorship of the two Committees remained unassailable, until they fell out amongst themselves. In April the Committee of Public Safety set up its own police bureau, with Robespierre in charge, to prosecute dishonest officials. The Committee of General Security deeply resented this interference with its own control of internal security, so that the two Committees became rivals rather than allies. There were also conflicts within the Committee of Public Safety. Some members disliked Saint-Just's Laws of Ventose and made sure they were never put into practice. Billaud and Collot had been closely attached to Hébert and so felt threatened by Robespierre. This applied especially to Collot, whose excesses at Lyon Robespierre had criticised.

e) The Coup of Thermidor

At this time of division, Robespierre disappeared for over a month from public life. He made no speeches in the Convention between 18 June and 26 July and only two at the Jacobin Club between 11 June and 9 July. He attended the Committee of Public Safety only two or three times and even gave up his work at the bureau of police. It may be that he was worn out, both physically and emotionally, as all the members of the Committee had worked long hours for months without a break. When he did surface it was to address the Convention, not the Committee. On 26 July (8 Thermidor) he abandoned his usual caution and made a speech attacking his colleagues. It was one of his worst speeches, which has been described as the rambling of an exhausted man who no longer knew where he was going. He finished by saying:

1 Let us recognise that there is a conspiracy against public liberty; that it derives its strength from a criminal coalition intriguing in the heart of the Convention itself; that this coalition has accomplices within the Committee of General Security and its bureaux; . . . that members of
5 the Committee of Public Safety have entered into the plot . . . What is the remedy? To punish the traitors.

When he was asked to name the men he was accusing, he declined. This refusal proved to be Robespierre's undoing. Moderates like

An Anti Robespierre cartoon claiming that most of the victims of the Terror were not from the privileged orders but were ordinary people.

Carnot and terrorists like Fouché and Collot all felt threatened, so they joined together to plot against Robespierre. When Robespierre attempted to speak on 9 Thermidor (27 July) he was shouted down. The Convention then voted for the arrest of Robespierre, his brother, Couthon and Saint-Just. As they were taken to prisons controlled by the Commune, they were soon released and gathered at the City Hall. The leaders of the Commune now called for an insurrection to support Robespierre and his colleagues. They ordered the National Guard of the Sections, still under their control, to mobilise. However, neither the Jacobin Club nor the Commune could mobilise these militants as they had done on 5 September 1793, because of the dictatorship established by the two Committees. The Committee of General Security now controlled the revolutionary committees of the Sections and the popular societies had been dissolved.

There was great confusion on the evening of 27 July, as the Convention was also calling on the National Guard to support it against the Commune. Most Sections took no action at first: only 16 sent troops to support the Commune. Yet they included some of the famous artillery units and for several hours the Commander of the National Guard had the Convention at his mercy. Only a failure of nerve by him and by Robespierre saved the Convention. Robespierre had no faith in a popular rising for which no plans had been made and wanted to keep within the law. Whilst he waited passively, the Convention outlawed those deputies whose arrest they had previously ordered, and the leaders of the Commune. This meant that they could be executed without a trial. The decree of outlawry persuaded many Sections to support the Convention. When they reached the *Hôtel de Ville* they found there was no-one defending it. Robespierre was arrested and on 28 July he and 21 others were executed. In the next few days over 100 members of the Commune followed Robespierre to the scaffold. The 'Terror' was dead, although the violence would continue. 'It had thrown back the invaders and laid the foundations for future conquests. In doing so it had preserved the heritage of 1789 for posterity'.[12]

4 The Significance of Robespierre

KEY ISSUE Was Robespierre a moderate or an extremist?

Robespierre remains the most controversial figure of the revolutionary period. Assessments of this complex politician differ widely. On the one hand, he is considered to be a power-crazed dictator who ruthlessly sent enemies and former allies to the guillotine, beyond the point when the threat to the republic had been removed. On the other hand, Robespierre is the 'Incorruptible' visionary of the revolution who sought to establish a republic of virtue based on equality.

Many of his ideas were commonplace among the Montagnards. He was not a great orator and his speeches were frequently long and repetitive. Unlike Danton, he could not dominate the Convention by the force of his personality. Richard Cobb described him as a 'prissy, vaguely ridiculous, prickly little man . . . no outstanding genius, a consistent winner of second prizes'.

Colin Lucas notes that Robespierre's reputation remains a mystery. 'We still do not know how this man, who never really held power, managed to build up such a reputation that his name was familiar all over France'. He never led or controlled either the Montagnards or the Committee. The Committee had no chairman and all its decisions were taken in common – Robespierre was one of 12 equal members. He was not even the main speaker for the Committee in the Convention. Barère filled that role. However, he was one of only two members of the Committee who never left Paris (many spent long periods away as representatives-on-mission or, like Carnot, at the front), and may, therefore, have played a more prominent role than most in the decisions of the Committee. But there is no documentary proof of this because the Committee did not keep minutes of its meetings.

Why, then, given his perceived limitations and his clear role in the Terror, is Robespierre admired? He certainly had a reputation as the champion of popular sovereignty and the liberties of the people. It has been suggested that Robespierre invented militant politics – the process by which a minority of activists can impose its will on a lazy majority.[13] He was genuinely popular particularly with the *sansculottes*. In the elections to the Convention he came top of the Paris list, gaining more votes than either Danton or Marat. For some, Robespierre was the sincere democrat who opposed the distinction between 'active' and 'passive' citizens. He thought that deputies and officials should be both accountable for their actions and subject to public scrutiny. That is why he wanted to set up a special police department, which would ensure that public officials did not abuse their powers. Yet, when he was in office, he did nothing to promote social and democratic policies.

He is often thought of as a bloodthirsty fanatic, dispatching all his opponents to the guillotine. The Law of Prairial, which he and Couthon proposed and which led to the Great Terror, is put forward as evidence of this. Yet Robespierre protected the 73 Girondins who had protested against the purge of the Convention on 2 June 1793, when many Jacobins wanted them executed. He publicly condemned the excesses of Collot and Fouché at Lyon, although he had demanded more severity after Couthon's moderate repression.

A good case can be made out for regarding Robespierre as a moderate. There was one criterion which he applied to all that he did: would his actions preserve the Revolution? If extremists were creating enemies of the Revolution, then they must be stopped. He denounced Hébert and the atrocities of representatives-on-mission because they were producing so many opponents of the Republic. He was in favour of relaxing the Maximum in the spring of 1794 because he realised that the regime could not wage war on the whole countryside. He condemned dechristianisation because of its political effects – it turned the peasants against the government. He was even prepared to be surprisingly indulgent towards the weaknesses of others. Private vices could be disregarded when they were not a threat to the regime. He was the most reluctant of all the members of the Committee of Public Safety to sacrifice Danton.

Was Robespierre the great revolutionary who directed events and caused them to take place? It was on his initiative that the Revolutionary Tribunal and Committee of Public Safety were set up and that the Law of Prairial was passed. Although he took no direct part in the *journée* of 2 June 1793, he was behind it. The threats to the existence of the Revolution in the spring of 1793 – foreign invasion, civil war and economic crisis – had been removed or brought under control by the end of the year. But this was the work of the Committee as a whole and it appears that other members played a larger part than Robespierre in bringing this about. Carnot, for example, was largely responsible for organising the successful prosecution of the war. It may be that Robespierre is often used as shorthand for the Committee of Public Safety and that when we talk about Robespierre's achievements we should be talking about those of the Committee.

Francois Furet sees Robespierre as a prophet, who believed everything he said and expressed it in the language of the revolution. His speeches were totally bound up with action '. . . the defence of equality, virtue or the people was the same thing as the conquest or exercise of power'.[14] Now there is a greater appreciation of his positive contribution to the revolution. Marc Bouloiseau sums him up well: 'He was a man of his times, of the Enlightenment, a patriot, a man with a sense of duty and of sacrifice, whose influence remains considerable'.[15] In France Robespierre's role during the revolution and his legacy remains controversial. While there are civic memorials to Danton in Paris, there are none to Robespierre. In St Petersburg, birthplace of the 1917 Russian revolution, he is honoured. A street along the banks of the Neva bears his name.

References

1 F. Furet and D. Richet, *The French Revolution* (London, 1970).
2 Richard Cobb, quoted in Andrew Hardman, *Nineteenth Century Europe* (London, 1976), p. 18.
3 Gwyn A. Williams, *Artisans and Sans-Culottes* (London, 1989), p. 19.
4 D.G. Wright, *Revolution and Terror in France 1789–1795* (Longman,1974), p. 115.
5 For the manifesto of the 'Enragés' see Hardman *op. cit.* pp. 172–175.

6 Richard Cobb, *The People's Armies* (Yale,1987), p. 21.
7 Josh Brooman *The Reign of Terror in France. Jean-Baptiste Carrier and the Drownings at Nantes* (Longman, 1986), p. 5.
8 See Colin Jones, *op. cit.* pp.119–120.
9 Douglas Johnson, 'Winds of Change' in *History Today* (May 1989), vol. 35 p. 5.
10 John McManners, *The French Revolution and the Church* (SPCK London,1969), p. 86.
11 Nigel Aston, *Religion and Revolution in France 1780–1804* (Macmillan, 2000), p. 259.
12 Norman Hampson, *The Terror in the French Revolution* (Historical Association, 1981), p. 31
13 John Hardman, *Robespierre* (Longman, 1999), p. 214.
14 François Furet, *Interpreting the French Revolution* (Cambridge, 1988), p. 59.
15 Marc Bouloiseau, *The New Encyclopedia Britannica* (Chicago, 1986) Vol. 10 p. 111.

Summary Diagram
Government by Terror: 1793–4

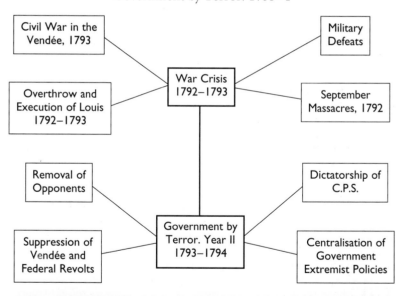

Working on Chapter 5

This chapter covers some of the most dramatic events of the whole of the revolutionary period. It is important that you understand how and why, when the Republic was under threat, the revolutionary government adopted the ruthless policies which it did, to defeat its enemies. An understanding of the impact of the war is very important. You may well find the struggle between the various factions complicated and difficult to understand. In your notes try to identify each one, and explain briefly its demands. Also try and evaluate the success of the policies passed by the revolutionary government. When reading the Chapter keep the following questions in mind:

- What pressures drove the revolution to become more extreme?
- To what extent did the policies which were passed help defend the republic?
- Was the policy of government by terror ultimately justified?

Answering structured questions and essay questions on Chapter 5

This extreme phase of the revolution is characterised by the emergence of France's strongest government since the *ancien régime*. It also considers the best known and most controversial figure of the revolution – Maximilian Robespierre. The usual approach with structured questions is to ask a relatively straightforward first part, followed by more demanding questions later. Look at the following examples:

1   **a)** Explain briefly who the *sans-culottes* were. (*4 marks*)
  b) In what ways did the popular movement influence the course of the revolution? (*6 marks*)
  c) To what extent were the demands of the *sans-culottes* met? (*10 marks*)
2   **a)** Explain briefly why the terror emerged in 1793. (*4 marks*)
  b) In what ways did the terror mark a turning point in the revolution? (*6 marks*)
  c) To what extent was the Terror supported by the population of France? (*10 marks*)

The following are examples of essay questions.

1   To what extent was the war responsible for the emergence of government by terror during 1793?
2   'The Terror was more than a response to a military crisis'. How valid is this interpretation of the revolutionary governments policies in 1793–4?
3   'His enemies were more powerful than his friends'. Assess this explanation of why Robespierre was unable to retain power in 1794?
4   Did the success of the Committee of Public Safety in solving France's problems make its downfall certain?

When, for example, you are making a plan to answer question 4, draw up a list of the problems which the Committee faced. Opposite each one note the extent to which it dealt with the problem successfully. Now list the reasons for the downfall of the Committee. What connection do they have with its successes?

Answering Source-based questions on Chapter 5

1 Robespierre

Read and examine the sources on pages 88–9 and 90. Answer the following questions:

a) What does Robespierre mean by 'civil liberty' (page 88, line 14) and 'factions which threaten it' (page 88, lines 18–19)? (*4 marks*)

b) How does Robespierre attempt to justify the conduct of Revolutionary Government? (*6 marks*)

c) In what ways do the two sources differ in their view of the Terror? (*10 marks*)

2 The Great Terror

Examine carefully the cartoon on page 95 and read the comments by Ruault on page 93. Then answer the following questions:

a) Explain the meaning of 'the horror and frequency of executions' (line 14) (*4 marks*)

b) How reliable are the two sources as evidence of the great terror? (*6 marks*)

c) To what extent do the sources provide an understanding of why the policy of government by terror was opposed? (*10 marks*)

Part (c) of each question is asking you to evaluate the sources either regarding their differences or their contribution to understanding much wider issues. It is important that you are critical in your response. Stress limitations as well as strengths.

The Thermidorian Reaction and the Directory 1794–9

6

POINTS TO CONSIDER

This chapter deals with what might appear to be less dramatic and less significant events than the Terror. However, do not underestimate this period. It was the longest lasting of the revolutionary regimes. As you read the chapter note the reaction to the Terror and the structure of the new system which replaced it. You will also need to gather together ideas on why the Directory failed and whether it achieved anything. Note also the course of the war. The Directory marks the emergence of Napoleon Bonaparte as a military figure who turned the direction of war in favour of France. Examine closely the events which led to the coup of Brumaire and the ultimate overthrow of the republic.

KEY DATES

1794 Aug Law of 22 Prairial repealed(1st), government reorganised
     Sept Church and State separated
     Nov Jacobin Club closed (12th)
1795 Apr Germinal Uprising (1st-2nd)
     May Prairial Uprising (20th-23rd)
     Aug Constitution of Year III (22nd)
     Oct Vendémiaire Uprising (1st), Bonaparte appointed
           commander of the Army of the Interior
     Nov Directory established (2nd)
1796 Mar Bonaparte appointed commander in Italy (11th)
1797 Sept Coup d'état of Fructidor (4th)
1798 May Coup d'état of Floréal (11th)
1799 Jun Coup d'état of Prairial (18th)
     Nov Bonaparte overthrows the Directory (9th–10th) 18–19
           Brumaire
     Dec Constitution of Year VII (25th)

1 The Thermidorian Reaction

> **KEY ISSUE** What reaction was there to the ending of the Terror?

There was a great outburst of delight and relief when Robespierre was executed. Charles de Lacretelle reported the reactions in Paris: 'People were hugging each other in the streets and at places of entertainment and they were so surprised to find themselves still alive that their joy almost turned to frenzy'. As William Doyle notes ; 'The ninth of Thermidor marked not so much the overthrow of one man or group of men as the rejection of a form of government.'[1]

Those who helped to overthrow Robespierre were known as the Thermidorians. They were a mixed group – members of the two great Committees, ex-terrorists and deputies of the Plain. The Plain now emerged from obscurity to take control. They were the men who had gained from the Revolution by buying *biens nationaux* (land) or by obtaining government contracts. As regicides (those who helped condemn Louis XVI to death) they were firmly attached to the Republic and did not want to see the return of a monarchy, even a constitutional one. They also disliked the Jacobins, who had given too much power to the *sans-culottes* and had interfered with a free market with the maximum laws. For them popular democracy, anarchy and the Terror were synonymous. They were joined by many Montagnards, which left the Jacobins a small silent minority in the Convention.

a) The Terror Ends

The Convention now set about dismantling the machinery of the Terror. Between the end of July 1794 and 31 May 1795, when the Revolutionary Tribunal was abolished, only 63 people were executed, including some who had been leading terrorists. Suspects were released from prison, the law of Prairial was repealed and the Jacobin Club was closed. The deputies were determined to gain control of the institutions which had made the Terror possible. This meant abandoning the centralisation established by the Committee of Public Safety. They decreed that 25 per cent of the members of the two Committees had to be changed each month. In August 16 committees of the Convention were set up to take over most of the work of the Committees of General Security and Public Safety The latter was now confined to running the war and diplomacy. In Paris the Commune was abolished. In local government power passed again to the moderates and property owners, who had been in control before June 1793.

The Thermidorians also decided to deal with religious issues by renouncing the Constitutional Church. In September 1794 the Convention decided that it would no longer pay clerical salaries, thus formally separating Church and State for the first time. State recognition of the Cult of the Supreme being was also ended. The free exercise of all religions was guaranteed in February 1795, although all outward signs of rebellion like clerical dress and the use of church bells were forbidden.

b) The Risings of Germinal and Prairial

The Thermidorians wanted to get rid of price controls, partly because they believed in a free market and partly because they were unenforceable. They were abolished in December 1794. Public arms workshops were closed or restored to private ownership. The result was a fall in the value of the *assignat* and massive inflation. The government had to buy its war materials at market prices. It therefore decided to print more *assignats* to pay for them. In August 1794, before the Maximum was abolished, the *assignat* was 34 per cent of its 1790 value. It dropped to 8 per cent in April 1795 and 4 per cent in May. The situation was made worse by a poor harvest in 1794. Grain shortages led to a huge increase in the price of bread.

The winter of 1794–5 was one of unprecedented severity. Rivers froze and factories closed down. A combination of economic collapse and the cold produced an enormous increase in misery, suicides and death from malnutrition, as scarcity turned into famine. Ruault described the situation.

> 1 The flour intended for Paris is stopped on the way and stolen by citizens even hungrier no doubt than ourselves, if such there be within the whole republic. Yet there is no lack of corn anywhere! There is still plenty in store in the departments of the Nord, etc. The farmers
> 5 absolutely refused to sell it for paper money; you have to go to them and take linen or table silver, jewellery or gold crosses, to get a few bushels. Discord sits more firmly than ever within the Convention. Now we are back to where we were at the end of April '93, and a hundred times worse as far as financial matters go. Too many *assig-*
> 10 *nats*, too much government slackness, too much favour shown to enemies of democracy, too much harshness and cruelty to former patriots.

The hungry turned their fury against the Convention. Germinal (1 April) was a demonstration rather than a rising. About 10,000 unarmed people poured into the Convention and demanded bread, the Constitution of 1793 and the release of imprisoned patriots. They expected support from the Montagnards in the Assembly but they did not receive any. When loyal National Guards appeared, the insurgents withdrew without offering any resistance. The repression which followed was light. Barère, Collot and Billaud, all former members of the great Committee of Public Safety, were sentenced to deportation and all known activists during the Terror were disarmed. During the spring of 1795, disillusionment with the Convention's inability to resolve the famine led to sporadic outbreaks of violence in the provinces. Some of the violence was organized by royalists.

Prairial was a much more serious affair. It was an armed rising like those of 10 August 1792 and 2 June 1793. On 1 Prairial (20 May 1795) hunger riots led to an invasion of the Convention by housewives followed by some National Guards. There was complete chaos for three hours, until the Montagnard deputies persuaded the Convention to pass decrees releasing patriots and setting up a Food

Commission. In the evening loyal National Guards arrived and cleared the Assembly. The next day about 20,000 National Guards surrounded the Convention. They were opposed by about 40,000 loyal Guards. The Convention's gunners went over to the rebels and aimed their cannon at the Assembly, but no-one was prepared to fire. The rebels presented their petition peacefully and then retired, after the President of the Convention had made some vague promises. On 3 Prairial (22 May) the Convention took the offensive. The rebel suburbs were surrounded by 20,000 troops of the regular army who forced them to give up their arms and cannon. This time the repression was severe: 40 Montagnards were arrested and six were executed. A military commission condemned to death a further 36, including the gunners who had gone over to the rebel side. About 6,000 militants were disarmed and arrested. Prairial marked the end of the *sans-culottes* as a political and military force. The significance of Prairial for Soboul was that the Revolution's mainspring had been smashed: 'the Revolution was at an end'.[2] – meaning the radical popular phase. No longer would they be able to threaten and intimidate an elected assembly. In Year IV conditions were just about as bad as in Year III, yet there was no rising. Demoralised, without arms and without leaders, the *sans-culottes* were a spent force.

Why had they failed? Partly because they were divided – the National Guard of several Sections was loyal to the Convention – partly because there was no institution like the Paris Commune in 1792 to co-ordinate their activities, and partly because they were politically inexperienced. When they had the advantage and had surrounded the Convention they allowed the opportunity to slip. Loss of support from the radical bourgeoisie, which they had enjoyed between 1789 and 1793 was crucial. The role of the army was a key factor – the regular army was used against the citizens of Paris for the first time since the Réveillon riots in the spring of 1789. Its intervention was decisive and made clear just how dependent the new regime was on the army. It was not the last time the army would interfere in France's internal politics.

c) The White Terror

The 'White Terror' was an attack on ex-terrorists and all who had done well out of the Revolution by those who had formerly been persecuted. White was the colour of the Bourbons, so 'White Terror' implies that it was a royalist movement. This was true in part, as returned *émigrés* and non-juring priests sought to take advantage of the anti-Jacobin revulsion at the persecution of the Year II. In Nîmes 'Companies of the Sun' were formed by royalists to attack former terrorists. However, most of those who took part in the White Terror were not royalists and had no intention of restoring

the composition of the Directory only by replacing the one director who retired each year with its own candidate. Martin Lyons assessment is, 'The Constitution enforced a rigid separation of powers. It permitted the legislature, if dominated by a hostile majority to paralyse the Directory. The Directory, which had no power of dissolution, and no veto, could only reply by unconstitutional methods.'[4]

As the Convention knew that it was unpopular and feared that free elections might produce a royalist majority, it decreed that two-thirds of the deputies in the Councils must be chosen from the existing deputies of the Convention. The Convention announced on the 1 Vendemiaire that the new Constitution had been approved in a plebiscite (a popular vote). Published figures showed that 1,057,390 were in favour of the Constitution, against 49,978 who opposed it. Four million voters did not vote. The Two-Thirds decree was accepted by only 205,000 to 108,000.

e) The Rising of Vendémiaire, 5 October 1795

The constitutional monarchists, who wanted a return to a limited monarchy like that in the 1791 Constitution, had been gaining public support, as they seemed to offer a return to stability. They had hoped to put Louis XVI's son, a prisoner in the Temple (one of prisons in Paris), on the throne but he died in June. From Northern Italy the Comte de Provence, Louis XVI's brother, immediately proclaimed himself Louis XVIII and on 24 June issued the Verona Declaration. The Declaration was a reactionary document, which made the task of restoring the monarchy more difficult. Louis promised to restore the 'ancient constitution' of France completely, which meant restoring the three orders and the *parlements*. He also promised to restore 'stolen properties', like that of the Church and the *émigrés*. This antagonised all those who had bought *biens nationaux* and all who had benefited from the abolition of the tithe and seigneurial dues. It was a great boost to the Republic.

In the capital open rebellion broke out on 5 October (13 Vendémiaire), when 25,000 armed Parisians gathered to march on the Convention. They greatly outnumbered the 7,800 government troops but the latter had cannon, under the command of General Bonaparte, whereas the rebels did not. The devastating artillery fire – Bonaparte's famous 'Whiff of grapeshot' – crushed the rebellion.[5] As over 300 were killed or wounded in the fighting, this was one of the bloodiest of the revolutionary *journées*. It also marked another watershed – the people of Paris would not again attempt to intimidate an elected assembly until 1830.

The divisions among the royalists and the unpopularity of the Verona Declaration all make the rising of Vendémiaire very mysterious. It is usually presented as a royalist rising brought about by the Two-Thirds Decree which, it is said, prevented the royalists from obtaining a majority in the elections to the Councils. Yet, the largest groups of rebels were artisans and apprentices: a third of those arrested were manual workers. The rising was not simply against the Two-Thirds Decree but had economic origins too, as many people, including *rentiers* – small proprietors – and government employees had been badly hit by inflation. A government agent reported on 16 July:

1 'The worker's wage is far too low to meet his daily needs; the unfortunate rentier, in order to keep alive, has to sell his last stick of furniture . . . the proprietor, lacking other means of subsistence, eats up his capital as well as his income; the civil servant, who is entirely dependent on
5 his salary, also suffers the torments of privation.'

These people, who were among the rebels, had supported the Thermidorians and defended the Convention in the risings of Germinal and Prairial.

The repression which followed was light. Only two people were executed, although steps were taken to prevent further risings. The Sectional Assemblies were abolished and the National Guard was put under the control of the new general of the Army of the Interior, Napoleon Bonaparte. For the second time in six months the army had saved the Thermidorian Republic.

2 The Directory

> **KEY ISSUES** What problems did the Directory face? Were there any achievements? Why was the Directory overthrown?

The new third elected to the Council after Vendémiaire and the dissolution of the Convention was mainly royalist, but it was unable to influence the choice of directors. As the Verona Declaration had threatened to punish all regicides, the *conventionnels* elected directors (Carnot was the best known) all of whom were regicides, as this would be a guarantee against a royalist restoration. The directors wanted to provide a stable and liberal government, which would maintain the gains of the Revolution. Yet the problems they faced were daunting. The war appeared to be endless, and it had to be paid for. The treasury was empty, taxes were unpaid and the *assignat* had plummeted in value. Many Frenchmen did not expect the Directory to last more than a few months. However, it did survive and for longer than any of the other revolutionary regimes. This was partly because it was committed to restore the rule of law and because its opponents were discredited. Few wanted a return either to the Jacobin Terror of Year II or to the absolute monarchy of the *ancien régime*. Many were prepared to accept a constitutional monarchy with limited powers but the royalists were divided amongst themselves. The extremists, who supported the Verona Declaration, hated the constitutional monarchists even more than the republicans. Public apathy also helped the Directory to survive – after six years of revolution and three years of war, revolutionary enthusiasm had all but disappeared. The army supported the Directory, as a royalist restoration would mean an end to the war. Army officers did not wish to be deprived of any opportunity provided by war for promotion or plunder. It was the army above all which enabled the Directory to overcome all challenges to its authority, but this was a double-edged weapon. The army which kept the Directory in power would be the most serious threat to its survival, if it became dissatisfied.

a) The Babeuf Plot, 1796

The first real challenge to the Directory came from Gracchus Babeuf. Babeuf disliked the Constitution of the Year III, because it gave power to the wealthy. He believed that the aim of society should be 'the common happiness', and that the Revolution should secure the equal enjoyment of life's blessings for all. He thought that as private property produced inequality, the only way to establish real equality was 'to establish the communal management of property and abolish private possession'. These ideas were much more radical than those put forward in the Year II and have led many historians to regard Babeuf as the first communist.[6] He was novel too in the way he thought of organising his Conspiracy of Equals. A rising, Babeuf realised, would not come about spontaneously but must be prepared by a small group of dedicated revolutionaries. Through propaganda and agitation they would persuade key institution like the army and police, who would provide the armed force to seize power, to support them. After seizing power, the revolutionary leaders should not hand it over to an elected assembly but should establish a dictatorship, in order to make fundamental changes in the organisation of society. Marxist historians like Soboul see Babeuf's importance in their theories by arguing that through Buonarotti (a fellow conspirator) his ideas passed to Blanqui in the nineteenth century and then to Lenin.

Babeuf's importance in the French Revolution itself was slight. His plot to overthrow the Directory was soon revealed by another conspirator. He received no support from the *sans-culottes* and little from former Jacobins. He was arrested in May 1796 and, with one other member of the Conspiracy, was executed a year later.

b) The *Coup d'État* of Fructidor, 1797

The elections of 1797 revealed a growing shift towards the monarchists. People were tired of war abroad and religious conflict at home and found the idea of a constitutional monarchy attractive, believing that it would offer peace and stability. Of the 216 ex-members of the

Convention who sought re-election, only 11 were returned. Monarchists won 180 of the 260 seats being contested, bringing their numbers to 330 in the Councils. The wealthy, populous northern departments returned the largest proportion of monarchists, which suggests that the Directory had lost the support of the richer bourgeoisie. The elections, in which fewer than ten per cent of electors voted in some departments, did not give the monarchists a majority in the Councils. However, they did mean that the Directory no longer had majority support and could rely on no more than a third of the deputies. All the monarchists needed to do, it appeared, was to wait for the next elections when more *conventionnels* would have to give up their seats. The monarchists could then obtain a majority and be in a position to restore a monarchy legally. The opponents of the Directory were also successful in elections to the provincial administrations.

The royalists showed their strength when the Councils appointed three of their supporters to important positions. One was elected President of the Five Hundred and another President of the Ancients. Barthélemy, the new director, was regarded as sympathetic to the monarchists, as was Carnot. Carnot was a moderate, who was prepared to give up conquered territory to make a lasting peace and so was disliked by the generals. This left only two directors who were fervent republicans. They were determined to prevent a royalist restoration and sought help from the army. Bonaparte had already sent Augereau to Paris with some troops to support the republican directors. On the night of 3–4 September 1797 (17–18 Fructidor, Year V) they ordered troops to seize all the strong points in Paris and surround the Council chambers. They then ordered the arrest of two directors, Carnot and Barthélemy, and 53 deputies.

The few deputies who attended the Councils after the *coup* showed that they were thoroughly frightened, when they approved of two laws demanded by the remaining directors. One annulled the elections in 49 departments, removing 177 deputies without providing for their replacement. Normandy, Brittany, the Paris area, and the north now had no parliamentary representation at all. A second decree provided for the deportation to the penal settlements in Guiana of Carnot (who had escaped and fled abroad), Barthélemy, the 53 deputies arrested, and some leading royalists. The directors also cancelled the local government elections and made appointments themselves. It was clear to all that this was the end of parliamentary government and of the Constitution of the Year III, and that the executive had won an important victory over the legislature. It also meant that the Directory could govern without facing hostile Councils.

After Fructidor, the new Directory took action against *émigrés* and refractory priests. *Émigrés* who had returned to France were given two weeks to leave: otherwise they would be executed. During the next few months many were hunted down and were sentenced to death.

Clergy were now required to take an oath of hatred for royalty: those refusing would be deported to Guiana. 1,400 non-juring priests were sentenced to deportation. The Terror which followed Fructidor was limited. It was carried out solely by the government and the army in an attempt to destroy the royalist movement. In the short-term it succeeded but, by alienating Catholic opinion, it provided more opponents for the Directory.

c) Financial Reform

Many of the monetary problems of the Directory were due to previous regimes, which had printed more and more *assignats* in order to pay for the war. As these were now almost worthless, in February 1796 the Directory issued a new paper currency, known as *mandats territoriaux*. They also soon lost value, and by July were worth less than five per cent of their nominal value. In February 1797 they ceased to be legal tender.

The monetary crisis had been catastrophic for government officials, *rentiers* and workers, as they saw a rapid decline in their purchasing power. Metal coins now became the only legal currency and these were in short supply: there were only one billion livres in circulation, compared with two and a half billion in 1789. This resulted in deflation, with prices dropping and credit becoming dearer. The inflation of 1795-7 had made the Directory unpopular with the workers. Now it became unpopular with businessmen.

From the *coup* of Fructidor to the spring of 1799 the Directory had little trouble with the purged Councils; Ramel, the Minister of Finance, had an opportunity to introduce some far-reaching reforms. In September 1797 two-thirds of the national debt was converted into bonds, which could be used to buy national property. This move was of immediate benefit to the government, as it reduced the annual interest on the national debt from 240 million francs (which was about a quarter of government expenditure) to 80 million. It was not of much use to the bondholders. Within a year the value of the bonds had fallen by 60 per cent and soon after that they became worthless, when the government refused to accept them for the purchase of *biens*. This was, in effect, a partial declaration of state bankruptcy, as two-thirds of the national debt was liquidated in this way. The ruin of the *rentiers* was completed, but the 'bankruptcy of the two-thirds' helped to stabilise French finances for a time. Aided by the smaller military expenditure when peace with Austria was made, Ramel was able to balance the budget for the first time since the Revolution began.

Ramel wanted to increase revenue as well as to cut expenditure. So, in 1798, he established four basic forms of direct taxation: a tax on trading licences, a land tax, one on movable property, and a new one on doors and windows. This was one of the most lasting achievements of the Directory and survived until 1914. At the same time, Ramel changed the method of collecting direct taxes, for which locally elected authorities had previously been responsible. Now central control was introduced: commissioners appointed by the directors were to assess and levy taxes.

As there was a continual deficit during wartime, the government had to fall back on practices of the old regime by reviving indirect taxes, although not the hated *gabelle* on salt. The *octrois* was imposed again and was very unpopular, as it raised the price of goods in the towns. Another source of income was plunder from those foreign states, especially in Italy and Germany, which had been occupied by French armies.

d) War: 1794–9

The battle of Fleurus in June 1794 was the first of a series of successes, which continued until all the members of the First Coalition except Britain had been knocked out of the war. In the summer of 1794, Belgium was occupied and, in the following winter, the United Provinces were invaded. The French conquered the Rhineland and crossed into Spain. Russia had intervened in Poland, which it was clear would be partitioned again. Prussia therefore made peace with France so that she would be free to claim Polish territory for herself. However, in fact, this made very little difference as Prussia had played little part in the war against France for the last year and a half. At the Treaty of Basle on 6 April 1795, Prussia promised to hand over its territories on the left bank of the Rhine to France. In return she would receive land on the right bank. This treaty freed French troops for an assault on her other enemies. Meanwhile, the United Provinces had become the Batavian Republic in January 1795, after a revolt against William V, who fled to England. Having lost Prussian support, the Dutch hastily made peace with France, whose ally they were compelled to become. The French hoped that the powerful Dutch navy would help to tip the naval balance against Great Britain. Spain too made peace in July, giving up to France her part of the island of San Domingo. Of the Great Powers, only Great Britain and Austria remained in the fight against France.

In 1796 the main French objective was to defeat Austria. Carnot drew up the plan of campaign and prepared a pincer movement against Austria. Armies under Jourdan and Moreau would march across Bavaria to Vienna, whilst the armies of the Alps and Italy would conquer Piedmont and Lombardy and then move across the Alps to Vienna. The main attack was to be that of Jourdan and Moreau, who were given 140,000 troops. The Italian campaign, under the 27-year-old General Bonaparte, was to play a secondary role. He had no field experience and had only 30,000 unpaid and ill-disciplined troops. Yet Napoleon was to turn Italy into the major battleground against Austria. He was able to do this by winning the loyalty of his men, to

France, 1789–95

whom he promised vast wealth. Within a month of taking command he had defeated Piedmont and forced her to make peace. In the same month of May he defeated the Austrians at Lodi and entered Milan. Mantua was the key to the passes over the Alps to Vienna, and Napoleon finally captured it in February 1797. The road to Vienna seemed open but all had not been going well for the French. The Archduke Charles had driven Moreau back to the Rhine, so Napoleon signed an armistice with Austria at Leoben in April.

Napoleon decided the terms at Leoben, without consulting the Directory. He was already confident enough to be making his own foreign policy and, in so doing, ignored specific instructions from the directors. They had wanted to use Lombardy as a bargaining counter to exchange for recognition of French control of the left bank of the Rhine. Napoleon joined Lombardy to Modena and the Papal Legations to form the Cisalpine Republic. Austria recognised Belgium, which the French had annexed in October 1795, as French territory. As compensation for giving up Lombardy and Belgium, Napoleon gave Austria Venice and part of the Venetian Republic, which provided access to the Adriatic. The fate of the left bank of the Rhine was unclear: it was to be decided by a Congress of the Holy Roman Empire. The Directory and the generals on the Rhine were furious that they had no choice but to accept what Napoleon had done. As the royalists had won the elections in France, the Directory knew it might need him. The peace of Campo Formio in October 1797 confirmed what had been agreed at Leoben.

Britain was now isolated. The French wanted to invade Britain, but for this to happen control of the seas was necessary. In particular they wanted to support Irish nationalists in their attempt to overthrow British rule in Ireland. The French hoped that with the aid of the Dutch and Spanish fleets (Spain had become an ally of France in October 1796) they would be able to obtain this. These plans were dashed by two British victories in 1797. In February the Spanish fleet was defeated off Cape St. Vincent and the Dutch fleet was almost completely destroyed at Camperdown in October. The war with Britain therefore continued.

On the continent the prospects for a permanent peace receded, as the French continued to extend their influence. The coup of Fructidor removed the two directors, Carnot and Barthélemy, who were prepared to return to France's old frontiers in order to gain a lasting peace. The directors now in control all wanted to keep French conquests and even to extend them. French foreign policy, therefore, became increasingly aggressive. Switzerland was important to France, as it controlled the most important passes to Italy. French troops entered Switzerland in January 1798 to help Swiss Patriots to seize power and turn Switzerland into the Helvetic Republic. Geneva was annexed to France. In Italy the Papal States were invaded and a Roman Republic was set up: the Pope fled to Tuscany. France had established 'sister' republics near her borders: three in Italy – the Cisalpine, Ligurian (which had replaced the Genoese Republic in June 1797) and Roman – plus the Batavian and Helvetic Republics. All were in effect satellite republics under French influence or control. Meanwhile the French were busy redrawing the map of Germany in negotiations with the Congress of the Holy Roman Empire at Rastatt. In March 1798 the Congress handed over the left bank of the Rhine to France and agreed that princes who had lost land there should be compensated by receiving church land elsewhere in Germany. 'The spring of 1798 marked the apex of the Revolution's power. In western, central and southern Europe, France had attained a degree of hegemony (domination) undreamed of even by Louis XIV.'[7] (see the map on page 114) From this position of great strength, the decline in French fortunes was equally dramatic. Within eighteen months the Directory would be overthrown.

Britain was the only country at war with France by 1798. Napoleon was put in command of the invasion army, but he abandoned this idea when France failed to gain command of the sea. Irish hopes of significant military support from France were also dashed. The small token force which was sent was easily defeated.[8] Napoleon decided instead to strike at Britain by invading Egypt. A French occupation of Egypt would interrupt British trade routes to India, would provide a base for a French expedition to India through the Red Sea and might persuade Indian princes to rise up against British rule. It would also enable France to control the eastern Mediterranean, and would provide both a market for French goods and a source of raw materials, especially cotton. In May 1798, Napoleon sailed from Toulon with 35,000 troops, captured Malta on the way and on 2 July arrived in Egypt. He captured Alexandria, defeated the Mamluks (former rulers of Egypt and Syria) at the battle of the Pyramids and went on to take Cairo, all in the same month. It was another brilliant and rapid campaign but was effectively ended on 1 August when Nelson captured or destroyed 11 out of 13 French ships of the line at Aboukir Bay. This left the French army stranded in Egypt.

The defeat of France at the battle of the Nile (also known as the battle of Aboukir Bay) encouraged other countries to take up arms against her again. A Second Coalition was formed, and Russia, which had not taken part in previous fighting against France, declared war in December. Tsar Paul was incensed at the French seizure of Malta, of which he had declared himself protector in 1797. France declared war on Austria in March 1799 because she allowed Russian troops to move through her territory. Immediately war resumed, France occupied the rest of Italy; Piedmont was annexed to France, and Naples was turned into another 'sister' republic – the Parthenopean. These early successes were followed by a series of defeats. The French were pushed back to the Rhine by the Austrians, and the Russians advanced through northern Italy. The French withdrew from the whole of Italy, except Genoa, as the Russians moved into Switzerland. It appeared that France would be invaded for the first time in six years, but, as had happened before, France was saved by quarrels among the allies. Austria, instead of supporting Russia in Switzerland, sent her best troops north to the Rhine. This allowed the French to move on to the offensive in Switzerland, where the Russians were compelled to withdraw in the autumn of 1799. The immediate danger to France was over.

e) The Revival of Jacobinism

The persecution of royalists since Fructidor had been severe, so they tended to keep away from the electoral assemblies in 1798. Although the Jacobins did well in the elections, they only managed to capture less than a third of the seats. The Directory could be sure of a majority in the new legislature, yet the directors persuaded the Councils by the Law of 22 Floréal (11 May) to annul the election of 127 deputies, 86 of whom were suspected Jacobins. The deputies to replace those not allowed to sit were largely chosen by the directors, another contravention of the 1795 Constitution. The *coup d'état* of Floréal was less drastic than that of Fructidor but it had less justification: no-one could pretend that the Republic was in danger. Once again the Directory had shown its contempt for the wishes of the electors.

By 1798 there were only 270,000 men in the French army, so Jourdan proposed that conscription should be re-introduced, for the first time since 1793. The Councils approved this in September 1798. However, it provoked widespread resistance. Much of Belgium, where conscription was also introduced, revolted in November and it took two months to put down the rising. Of the first draft of 230,000, only 74,000 reached the armies.

The 1799 elections once again showed the unpopularity of the Directory. Only 66 of 187 government candidates were elected. Among the rest there were about 50 Jacobins, including some who had been purged at Floréal. They were still a minority but many moderate deputies were now prepared to follow their lead. They had become disillusioned with the government, as news of military defeats reached Paris. The military situation was regarded as so desperate that the Councils were persuaded that emergency measures were needed and they passed laws proposed by Jacobins. In June 1799 Jourdan called for a new *levée en masse*: all men between 20 and 25 were to be called up immediately. Because the armies were being pushed back into France, the Republic could no longer pay for the war by foreign requisitions. A forced loan on the rich was therefore decreed, which was to raise 100 million livres and meant that the wealthy might have to give up as much as three-quarters of their income. The Law of Hostages of 12 July was even worse for the *notables*. Any areas resisting the new laws could be declared 'disturbed'. Local authorities could then arrest relatives of *émigrés*, nobles or rebels. They could be imprisoned, fined and their property confiscated to pay for the damage done by those causing disturbances. These measures seemed a return to the Terror of the Year II, when there had been arbitrary arrests and all the rich had been suspects, but still only 10 million livres of the forced loan had been collected by November. Conscription should have produced 402,000 troops but, as in 1798, there was widespread resistance and only 248,000 (60 per cent) joined the army. Many joined brigands or royalist rebels to avoid being called up. The Law of Hostages was hardly ever applied, because of opposition from local officials.

In 1799 there was a virtual collapse of government administration in the provinces. The Directory could not persuade local *notables* to accept office and had few troops to enforce its decrees. Local authorities were often taken over by royalists, who refused to levy forced loans, persecute non-juring priests or catch deserters. The National Guard was not large enough to keep order in the absence of regular troops, so substantial areas of the countryside were not policed at all. Brigandage was a result of the administrative collapse. By November 1799 there was civil war in the Ardèche: government commissioners were killed as quickly as they were replaced.

In the late summer of 1799 the military situation improved. The Russians were driven out of Switzerland in September. Sieyès, who had become a director, saw this as an opportunity to stage a *coup*. He wanted to strengthen the executive but knew that the Five Hundred would not agree to this and that it could not be done constitutionally. For a *coup* the support of the army was necessary. Who would be a reliable general? Moreau was approached but recommended Bonaparte, who had returned from Egypt on 10 October. 'There is your man', he told Sieyès. 'He will make your *coup d'état* far better than I can.'

f) Brumaire

On his way to Paris Bonaparte was greeted enthusiastically by the population, as the most successful of the republican generals and the one who had brought peace in 1797. He had made up his mind to play a leading role in French politics. He agreed to join Sieyès' *coup* but only on condition that a provisional government of three consuls, who would draft a new constitution, should be set up.

Sieyès wanted to move the Councils to St Cloud, as in Paris the Jacobins in the Five Hundred were numerous enough to provide opposition to his plans. The Ancients, using as an excuse a terrorist plot, persuaded the Councils to move to St Cloud. Once there it became clear on 19 Brumaire (10 November) that the only plot was one organised by Sieyès.

The Council of Five Hundred was furious, so Bonaparte reluctantly agreed to address both Councils. His appearance in the Five Hundred with armed grenadiers was greeted with cries of 'Outlaw' and 'Down

Bonaparte's 'Proclamation to the French Nation', 10 November 1799[9]

'On my return to Paris I found all authority in chaos and agreement only on the one truth that the constitution was half destroyed and incapable of preserving liberty. Men of every party came to see me, confided their plans, disclosed their secrets and asked for my support; I refused to be a man of party. The Council of the Ancients called upon me and I responded to its appeal. A plan for general reform has been drawn up by me upon whom the nation is accustomed to look as the defenders of liberty, equality and property. That plan needed calm examination, free from all fear and partisan influence. Therefore the Council of the Ancients resolved to transfer the legislative body to Saint-Cloud and charged me to deploy the force necessary to ensure its independence. I believed it my duty to my fellow-citizens, to the soldiers laying down their lives in our armies, to the national glory gained at the price of their blood to accept this command . . . Frenchmen, you will no doubt recognize in my conduct the zeal of a soldier of liberty and of a devoted citizen of the republic. Liberal, beneficent and traditional ideas have returned to their rightful place through the dispersal of the odious and despicable factions which sought to overawe the Councils'.

BONAPARTE

with the tyrant'. He was physically attacked by Jacobin deputies and had to be rescued by fellow officers. It was not at all clear that the soldiers would take action against the elected representatives of the nation. Napoleon's brother Lucien, President of the Five Hundred, came to his rescue when he told the troops that some deputies were trying to assassinate their general. At this they took action and cleared the hall where the 500 were meeting. A rump of the Councils then approved a decree abolishing the Directory and replacing it with a provisional executive committee of three members, including Sieyès and Napoleon. The great beneficiary of Brumaire was Napoleon but his brother was the true hero of the hour.

Paris remained calm, and this should be interpreted as a sign of apathy rather than of approval. 'In the provinces, where no preparatory measures had been taken by the conspirators, the reaction was varied. . . . There was a good deal of surprise, precious little exultation (rejoicing) and even some opposition.'[10] A poster in Paris showed how disillusioned many were with the Directory and what they hoped a change of regime would achieve:

1 France wants something great and long-lasting. Instability has been her
downfall, and she now invokes steadiness. She has no desire for a monarchy . . . but she does want unity in the action of the power executing laws.
She wants a free and independent legislature . . . She wants her repre-
5 sentatives to be peaceable conservatives, not unruly innovators. Finally,
she wants to enjoy the benefits accruing from ten years of sacrifices.

When Napoleon presented the new Constitution of year VIII to the
French people, on 15 December 1799 he said that it 'is founded on
the true principles of representative government, on the sacred rights
of property, equality and liberty. Citizens the revolution is established

A contemporary print which depicts France as a woman being dragged into
an abyss by two figures representing revolutionary fanaticism. Napoleon is
attempting to draw her back towards justice, unity, peace and plenty.

on the principles which began it. It is finished.'[11] Many did not realise the significance of the *coup d'état* of Brumaire. One phase of the revolution was over and another was beginning.

g) Why did the Directory fail?

The regime collapsed above all under the weight of its own contradictions: the contradictions of a liberal system which could only survive by violating its own legality, which needed war – at any rate since Fructidor – to satisfy the contractors and generals and to provide itself with income, and which, through war, alienated its freedom of manoeuvre and justified the accusations of its adversaries at home and abroad.[12]

The directors had wanted to produce a stable government, which maintained the gains of the Revolution of 1789 whilst avoiding the extremes of Jacobin dictatorship or royalism. Their failure to obtain stability was partly due to the Constitution of the Year III, with its annual elections. It made no provision for settling disputes between the executive and the legislature or for changing the Constitution in under nine years. The directors, therefore, interfered with the election results, to ensure they had a majority in the Councils. They purged the Councils in Fructidor 1797 and Floréal 1798. Napoleon told the Ancients that the Constitution had ceased to be observed: 'You yourselves destroyed it on 18 Fructidor, on 22 Floréal. . . . Nobody has any respect for it now.'

The Thermidorians had used the army to put down the risings of Prairial and Vendémiaire and the Directory had used it to carry out the *coup d'état* of Fructidor. To an extent, the Directory was dependent on the army and an army take-over was a distinct possibility. Yet it was not the generals who planned the *coup* of Brumaire. Once again they were called in by the politicians, who assumed that they would then leave the scene to the civilians as they had done after Fructidor.

Most of the people who would normally have supported the Directory – owners of *biens*, the wealthy notables – were alienated by its policies, especially its forced loans. They showed this by refusing, in increasingly large numbers, to vote in the annual elections or to take up posts in local government. The population as a whole was apathetic. Public inertia may have helped the Directory to survive but it meant that there was no-one prepared to defend it. People were listless and lacking in enthusiasm because the war had gone on for so long and they wanted peace above all. Yet war had become a necessity for the Directory. It needed war to keep ambitious generals and unruly soldiers out of France, to provide money for the French treasury and to produce the victories and the prestige which would enable the regime to survive. 'The Directory', wrote Napoleon while in exile on St Helena after 1815, 'was overpowered by its own weakness: to exist it needed a state of war as other governments need a state of peace.' One of the reasons for Napoleon's popularity was that he had brought peace at Campo Formio in 1797. After this, war could have been avoided on the continent but for the actions of the Directory in extending French influence in Italy and Switzerland and in its approval of the Egyptian expedition. This led to the formation of the Second Coalition, military defeats, risings against France in the conquered territories and further royalist activity in France. Renewed war also produced a flurry of Jacobin activity, including a forced loan and the Law of Hostages. The Jacobins were never more than an urban minority and were no direct threat to the Directory but, by reviving fears of a Terror like that of the Year II, they convinced many that the Directory could not, and should not, survive.

These events discredited the Directory and produced politicians who were not as attached to the republic as the *conventionnels* had been. Only 12 per cent of those elected to the Councils in 1799 had been members of the Convention and only five per cent were regicides. Over half the deputies chosen in 1799 were elected for the first time that year. These deputies were prepared to accept the view of Sieyès that the Constitution should be changed and that this involved getting rid of the Directory. They were not only prepared to welcome the new regime but took part in running it. Of 498 high officials of the Consulate 77 per cent had been deputies under the Directory. These men of the right and centre wanted stability and were prepared to accept an authoritarian regime to get it.

Did the Directory have any achievements? Despite the fact that the Directory was the longest lasting of the revolutionary regimes there has been a tendency to dismiss it as a period when very little was achieved. The trend in recent years has been to consider the period in a more balanced and objective way. Many of the achievements of the Consulate were initiated during the Directory. The financial reforms and reorganization of the tax system contributed to economic recovery. Changes in administration within the departments preceded the roles later taken by prefects. Industrial and agricultural expansion was underway and would develop much more fully during the Napoleonic era. Although its collapse was sudden, the Directory's achievements should not be dismissed as insignificant.

References

1 William Doyle, *op. cit.* p. 281.
2 Albert Soboul, *op. cit.* p. 447.
3 Francois Gendron, *The Gilded Youth of Thermidor* (McGill-Queens University Press, 1993) p. 206.
4 Martin Lyons, *France Under the Directory* (Cambridge, 1975) p. 20.
5 George Rudé, *Revolutionary Europe 1783–1815* (Fontana, 1964) p. 171.
6 R.B. Rose, *Gracchus Babeuf: The First Revolutionary Communist* (Edward Arnold, 1978).

7 T.C.W. Blanning, *The Origins of the French Revolutionary Wars* (Longman, 1986) p. 179.
8 Ian R. Christie, *Wars and Revolutions Britain 1760–1815* (Edward Arnold, 1982) p. 243–4.
9 Cited in E.G. Rayner and R.F. Stapley, *The French Revolution 1789–99* (Hodder & Stoughton, 1990) p. 76.
10 Malcolm Crook, *Napoleon Comes to Power* (University of Wales Press, 1998) p. 65.
11 Geoffrey Ellis, *Napoleon* (Longman, 1997) p. 37.
12 Denis Wornoff, *The Thermidorian Regime and the Directory 1794–1799* (Cambridge,1984) p. 192.

Summary Diagram
The Thermidorian Reaction and the Directory 1794–9

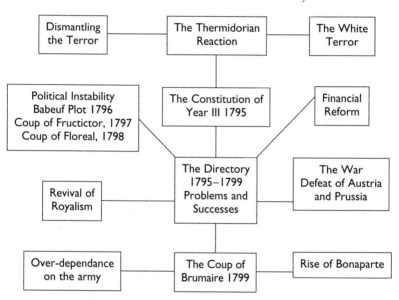

| Dismantling the Terror | The Thermidorian Reaction | The White Terror |

| Political Instability Babeuf Plot 1796 Coup of Fructictor, 1797 Coup of Floreal, 1798 | The Constitution of Year III 1795 | Financial Reform |

| Revival of Royalism | The Directory 1795–1799 Problems and Successes | The War Defeat of Austria and Prussia |

| Over-dependance on the army | The Coup of Brumaire 1799 | Rise of Bonaparte |

Working on Chapter 6

The Directory tends to be overshadowed by the Terror. However, it is a vital period not only because it was the longest lasting of the revolutionary regimes, but because it marks the emergence of Napoleon Bonaparte. When working on this Chapter you may find it helpful to consider the following questions: **i)** What was the Directory trying to achieve? **ii)** Why was it so unstable? **iii)** Did it achieve anything? and, of course, **iv)** Why was it overthrown? If you are following a course with an emphasis on the revolutionary war you should note carefully how and why the military fortunes of the Republic changed, in particular how the First Coalition was defeated and why the Second was formed. Pay close attention also to the emergence of Napoleon Bonaparte.

Answering structured questions and essay questions on Chapter 6

The most obvious theme to focus on when studying the Directory is why it was overthrown. However, you should also prepare yourself for other possible topics relating to the war, the Thermidorian reaction and successes achieved by the Directory. The following are two examples of structured questions:

1   **a)** Explain briefly who the Gilded Youth were. (*4 marks*)
    b) Why did the risings of Germinal and Prairial occur? (*6 marks*)
    c) To what extent did the Constitution of Year III create a 'Bourgeois republic'? (*10 marks*)
2   **a)** Outline briefly the new republics created by France between 1794 and 1798. (*4 marks*)
    b) What were the strengths and weaknesses of the French military during the Directory? (*6 marks*)
    c) To what extent was French military success due to the ability of her generals? (*10 marks*)

Structured questions will require you to display a range of skills, each of which will be linked to specific questions. The skills to be tested will usually consist of factual recall, explanation and analysis/evaluation. However, in an essay you will need to deploy all these skills, at various times, in one piece of continuous prose writing. A number of examples of essay questions on the Directory are given below:

1   'Few friends and many enemies'. How valid is this assessment of the Directory's failure to establish itself securely in France between 1795 and 1799?
2   'The Directory was designed to preserve the gains of the revolution.' Discuss
3   To what extent was the Directory totally dependant on the support of the army?
4   How valid is the view that the Directory's domestic achievements have been unjustly overshadowed by its successes in war?
5   'Disunity among its enemies was the reason France was able to survive against the other European powers'. How valid is this explanation of France's involvement in the revolutionary war?

These questions in the main require you to evaluate the proposition in the question against other contributory factors. When you are writing an essay a good introduction is essential. Your opening paragraph should form a bridge between the question and the answer and as such should contain a reference to the question. The core of your argument should form the bulk of the answer. Use paragraphs to develop your argument. While you will need to provide factual content try and avoid providing a narrative account. Always end your essay with a conclusion which draws together in summary form your response.

Source-based questions on Chapter 6

1 The Risings of 1795
Read carefully the report by Ruault on page 104 and that of a government agent on page 109. Answer the following questions:

a) Explain the following references:
   (i) 'Discord sits more firmly than ever within the Convention' (page 104, line 7) (*1 mark*)
   (ii) 'The worker's wage is far too low to meet his daily needs' (page 109, line 1) (*1 mark*)
b) What do the sources suggest are the problems facing ordinary people? (*4 marks*)
c) Comment on the reliability of the sources to an historian studying the problems of the Directory. (*6 marks*)
d) How far is it possible to agree with the view that economic factors were the main cause of opposition to the Directory? (*8 marks*)

2 The Coup of Brumaire
Read carefully the words of the poster on page 120, Napoleon's proclamation on page 119, and examine the print on page 120. Answer the following questions:

a) Explain the following references: 'I refused to be a man of party' (page 119, line 5) (*1 mark*)
   '... she wants to enjoy the benefits accruing from ten years of sacrifices.' (page 120, line 6) (*1 mark*)
b) What do the sources suggest are the weaknesses of the Directory? (*4 marks*)
c) Comment on the reliability of the three sources as evidence of the causes of the coup of Brumaire. (*6 marks*)
d) To what extent would you agree that the existence of factions were responsible for the overthrow of the Directory? (*8 marks*)

7 The Impact of the Revolution

POINTS TO CONSIDER

This chapter is very different from the others in that it attempts to provide an overview of the impact the Revolution had over a range of areas. These areas relate specifically to France and in general to Europe. They will include French society, the French economy, the nature of warfare, and Europe in general. In many ways you should view this chapter as a drawing together of the various strands which make up the revolution. It is best understood after you have studied and discussed the events of the revolutionary period. Some of the themes considered here could form the basis of synoptic type assessments which require an evaluation of how areas developed and changed over a period of time.

Contemporaries regarded the French Revolution as an event of major importance. The British ambassador in France, the Duke of Dorset, wrote to the government as early as 16 July 1789 about 'the greatest Revolution that we know anything of'. Yet some historians, particularly English and American, have tended subsequently to play down its significance. They maintain that many of the reforms which took place during the Revolution – free trade, religious toleration, the end of venal offices and financial privileges – were all taking place under the *ancien régime*. They woul§d have happened if there had been no Revolution. The rise of the bourgeoisie and the economic dominance of the British were also taking place before the Revolution and were not much affected by it. How true is this? In this chapter we shall be looking at what changes took place between 1789 and 1799 which were lasting, who in France gained and who lost from the Revolution, and what effect the Revolution had outside France.

1 The *Ancien Régime* Dismantled

KEY ISSUE What impact did the Revolution have on the institutions and social groupings of the *ancien régime*?

Most of the *cahiers* in 1789 were moderate and none suggested the abolition of the monarchy. Yet within a short time, beginning with the August Decrees and the Declaration of Rights, fundamental changes had taken place which swept away most of the institutions of the old regime. This had led historians, such as the American G.V. Taylor, to maintain that it was not the revolutionaries who made the Revolution but the Revolution which made the revolutionaries. 'The revolutionary state of mind', he wrote, 'expressed in the Declaration of the Rights of Man and the decrees of 1789–91 was a product – and not a cause – of a crisis that began in 1787'. The most famous of the abandoned institutions was the monarchy, abolished in 1792. However, this did not prove to be lasting, as the monarchy was restored in 1814, although it was not to be the same as in 1789. Its powers were to be limited, particularly by an elected assembly which had the right to pass laws. Assemblies during the Revolution were hardly democratic as, after the primary assemblies, voting was confined to a small minority of property-holders. An elected legislature was to be one of the permanent changes brought about by the Revolution.

The reforms of the Constituent Assembly were to prove, as a whole, the most radical and the most lasting of the Revolution. The France of the *ancien régime* was dismembered and then reconstructed according to new principles. Most of the institutions of the old regime were abolished, never to return. The legal distinction between Estates disappeared, as did the privileges of nobles, Church and *pays d'états* – although the nobility returned under Napoleon. The *généralités* and *intendants*, the old courts of law and the 13 *parlements* went too. The entire financial structure of the *ancien régime* was abandoned: direct taxes (the *taille, capitation* and *vingtième*); the Farmers-General; indirect taxes such as the *gabelle* and *aides*; internal customs; venal offices, and the guilds and corporations all came to an end, along with other restrictive practices. The Church was drastically transformed by losing the tithe and its lands. The sale of the *biens nationaux* was the greatest change in land ownership in France for hundreds of years: a tenth of the land came on to the market at one time.

What replaced all that had been destroyed? The administrative structure of modern France was established: the departments, districts and communes; new regular courts of law for both criminal and civil cases; a centralised treasury; taxes from which no-one was exempt and the standardisation of weights and measures through metrication. Careers became open to talent in the bureaucracy, the army and the Church. All this – both the destructive and constructive work – was largely achieved in two years and was to be lasting. It was a remarkable achievement.

The three Estates of the *ancien régime* were also affected by the Revolution, though the extent to which they suffered or benefited is a matter for debate amongst historians.

a) The Church

The church was one of the main losers in the Revolution. At an early stage it lost most of its wealth: its income from the tithe, its lands (which were taken over by the state) and its financial privileges, all of which were never recovered. Later its monopoly of education was removed, as was its control of poor relief and hospitals. The clergy became civil servants, as they were paid by the state, and many were better off, as they received higher salaries from the government than they had received before. Yet the Civil Constitution of the Clergy in 1790 produced a deep division within the Church. Those who did not accept it (about half the clergy) were persecuted as potential or actual counter-revolutionaries. Over 200 were killed in the September Massacres in 1792 and over 900 became official victims of the Terror. About 25,000 (a sixth of the clergy) emigrated or were deported. Many parishes were without a priest and, during the dechristianisation campaign of Year II, most churches were closed. Even the constitutional clergy were abandoned, when the government refused to pay any clerical salaries in 1794. It has been argued that, in those areas where the majority had taken the constitutional oath, the consequence was ' a lowering of esteem for religion which lasted well into the nineteenth century'.[1] The state was separated from the Church and was to remain so until Napoleon's Concordat with the Pope in 1802. This rift had the unfortunate effect of embittering relations between Church and state for much of the nineteenth century. Church leaders looked on republicans as terrorists and persecutors and became suspicious of any attempt at reform. Republicans looked on the Church as an institution determined to oppose change, and as such their main enemy, and wanted a return to the separation of Church and state. This would not be achieved until 1905.

b) The Nobility

Nobles were amongst the early leaders of the Revolution but withdrew from participation in public affairs after 1792. As individuals they were among the greatest losers from the Revolution. They lost their feudal dues and this in some areas could amount to 60 per cent of their income. 'We never recovered', wrote the Marquis de la Tour du Pin, 'from the blow to our fortune delivered on that night' (4 August 1789). They also lost their financial privileges and consequently paid more in taxation. The *vingtième* and *capitation* usually took about five per cent of their income: the new land tax on average took 16 per cent. They lost their venal offices, their domination of high offices in the army, Church and state and even their right to bequeath their estates undivided to their oldest son (inheritances had to be divided equally amongst sons). In 1790 the nobility was abolished. From the beginning of the Revolution some nobles emigrated, and eventually at least 16,500 went abroad (seven to eight per cent of all nobles). Property of those who emigrated was confiscated and this affected between a quarter and a half of all noble land. About 1,200 nobles were executed during the Terror and many were imprisoned for months as suspects. Nobles appear to have been the principal victims of the Revolution: many lost their lands and some lost their heads.

In recent years, this traditional picture has been revised and modified. It is now generally accepted that nobles who stayed in France and were not persecuted during the Terror (the majority) retained their lands and never lost their position of economic dominance. Napoleon's tax-lists show that nobles were still amongst the wealthiest people in France. For example, of the 30 biggest taxpayers on the Lozère in 1811, 26 were nobles. Under Napoleon many *émigré* nobles returned to France and began to buy back their lands. For example, in the Sarthe nobles had lost 100,000 acres but had recovered it all by 1830. Though precise statistics are not available for the whole of France, nobles overall may have recovered a quarter of the land they had lost. Members of the ruling political élite in France both before and after the Revolution were large landowners and high officials, both noble and bourgeois, who came to be called notables. Owing to the economic disruption caused by the Revolution, they continued to invest in land rather than industry, particularly when so much land came on to the market cheaply because of the sale of *biens nationaux*. Francis d'Ivernois asked what Frenchman was mad enough

1 To risk his fortune in a business enterprise, or in competition with foreign manufacturers? He would have to be satisfied with a profit of ten, or at most twelve per cent, while the state offers him the possibility of realising a return of thirty, forty or even fifty per cent, if he
5 places his money in one of the confiscated estates.

This group of notables governed France up to 1880 at least, and in this sense the *ancien régime* continued well into the nineteenth century.

c) The Bourgeoisie

Marxists have always said that the French Revolution was a bourgeois revolution. Albert Soboul maintained that 'The French revolution constitutes the crowning achievement of a long economic and social evolution that made the bourgeoisie the master of the world'.[2] He argued that businessmen and entrepreneurs assumed the dominant role hitherto occupied by inherited wealth. These men, with their willingness to take risks and their spirit of initiative, avoided speculation and invested their capital in production. They contributed in this way to the rise of industrial capitalism.

This interpretation has been challenged by a number of British and American historians. They point out that the bourgeoisie continued to invest in land rather than industry, just as they had done before the Revolution. There were few representatives of trade, finance or industry in the elected assemblies: 85 out of 648 deputies in the Constituent Assembly, 83 out of 891 in the Convention. Small in numbers, they did not take the lead in political affairs. There is no doubt that laws were passed which could eventually benefit the industrialist – the abolition of internal customs barriers, guilds and price controls, the prohibition of workers' associations and the introduction of a uniform system of weights and measures. Yet it was difficult to take advantage of these new laws until transport improved sufficiently to create a national market and this had to wait for the railways. Most merchants and manufacturers were worse off in 1799 than they had been in 1789. The French Revolution was not, therefore, either in its origins or its development, carried out by the mercantile and industrial bourgeoisie.

Yet the French Revolution *was* a bourgeois revolution, as the bourgeoisie were its main beneficiaries and provided all its leaders after 1791. Many of the reforms of the Constituent Assembly were supposed to apply to all citizens equally but only the bourgeoisie could take full advantage of them. Workers and peasants benefited little when careers became open to talent, as they were not educated. When the *biens* were put up for sale they were sold in large lots and this too benefited the middle classes, who owned between 30 and 40 per cent of French land by 1799. The voting system also favoured the bourgeoisie, as it was limited to property owners. Consequently, nearly all the members of the various assemblies were bourgeois, as were all the ministers. Most of the revolutionary bourgeoisie were lawyers. There were 166 of them in the Constituent Assembly, and another 278 members were public officials, most of whom had a legal training. In the Convention there were 241 lawyers and 227 officials. These were the people who gained most from the Revolution, as they had the training to take advantage of careers open to talent. When venal offices were abolished, it appeared that this group would suffer, as their compensation was based on the values of their offices in 1770 and they were paid in *assignats*, which soon depreciated. However, many were elected to new local and national offices, which paid well. The central administration employed under 700 officials in the 1780s but by 1794, owing to the war, this number had risen to 6,000. The number of officials in the country as a whole increased five-fold to about 250,000, about ten per cent of the bourgeoisie. Bourgeois had always filled the lower and middle ranks of the judiciary and the administration. With the Revolution they also took over the highest posts, which previously had all been held by nobles. Their dominance of the administration was to continue throughout the nineteenth century.

However, there were bourgeois who did not benefit from the Revolution, such as merchants of the Atlantic ports, manufacturers of luxury goods, and *rentiers*, who were paid in *assignats*, which lost most of their value. In 1797 rentiers lost most of their investments in Ramel's 'bankruptcy of the two-thirds'. Nevertheless, most bourgeois did well out of the Revolution and would accept only those regimes which promised to maintain their gains.

d) The Peasantry

It is almost impossible to divide peasants into separate categories: landowners, tenant farmers, sharecroppers and labourers. Although there were usually some of each in the villages, most peasants did not fall into any one group. The majority held some of their land freehold, rented other parts and from time to time sold their labour. The peasantry registered a mixture of gains and losses during the Revolution. Many lost their income from domestic industry, when there was a depression in textiles. Others saw their rents rise by as much as a quarter, when landlords were allowed to add the value of the abolished tithe to their rents. Conscription, in 1793 and again in 1798, affected all and, with dechristianisation in 1793–4, turned many peasants against the Revolution. Those who produced for the market were badly affected by the Maximum on the price of grain in the Year II and by the requisitions to feed the towns and the army. The result of all these measures was a widespread, popular resistance movement, which in the Vendée flared into open revolt. In Brittany and Normandy, where the abolition of feudalism produced few benefits as most peasants rented their land, there was *chouannerie*. In the south too there was widespread opposition, as the Revolution seemed to benefit the rich Protestants of towns like Nîmes rather than the local Catholics. In some areas this opposition was caught up in royalist counter-revolution but peasants generally did not wish to see a return to the *ancien régime*, which might bring with it a restoration of feudal dues. Their opposition was therefore anti-revolutionary rather than counter-revolutionary. They wanted stability, their old way of life and the exclusion of 'foreigners' (officials from Paris or from outside their own district) from their affairs. Resistance produced repression and executions – nearly 60 per cent of the official victims of the Terror were peasants or workers and many more were killed when the army devastated the Vendée.

Yet most peasants benefited in one way or another from the Revolution. All gained from the abolition of indirect taxes and their total tax burden was reduced. Those who owned land benefited from the abolition of feudal dues and the tithe. In the north and east, where the Church owned much land, peasants were able to buy some of the *biens*, though it was usually the richer peasants who were able to do this. In the south-west even share-croppers bought *biens* and became supporters of the Revolution. Peasants also gained from inflation, which grew steadily worse between 1792 and 1797. They were able to pay off their debts with depreciating *assignats* and tenants were able to redeem their leases. Judicial and local government reforms were to the advantage of all peasants. The abolition of seigneurial justice was a great boon, as it was replaced by a much fairer system. The Justice of the Peace in each *canton* provided cheap and impartial justice. The right of self-government granted to local authorities favoured the peasants too, especially at the municipal level, where councils were elected and filled by peasants. Over a million people took part in these councils in 1790 and many more later. In the north and east most of these were rich peasants, though in Poitou poorer peasants, tenant farmers and share-croppers took control. Peasants looked on municipal self-government as one of their greatest gains from the Revolution. Both the self-governing commune and Justices of the Peace survived to play important roles in the nineteenth century.

The poor peasants, the landless day-labourers and sharecroppers are usually regarded as sufferers from the Revolution. They did not benefit from the abolition of feudal dues and they were hit hard by the inflation from 1792 to 1797, as wages failed to rise as quickly as prices. Many relied on cottage industry for survival and when the market for this collapsed, they became destitute. However, not all was loss. They did gain from the abolition of indirect taxes. From 1797 to 1799 they gained from deflation, so that by 1799 their real wages were higher than they had been in 1789.

The Revolution, therefore, affected the peasants in different ways but for most (as for most bourgeois) their gains outweighed their losses, especially for those who owned land. Peter Jones concludes that: 'Those who managed to survive the dearths of the Revolution and the terrible famine of 1795, experienced a real improvement in purchasing power; the first such improvement in several generations.'[3] Lecointe-Puyraveau, a government commissioner in the Deux-Sèvres, summed up the impact of the Revolution on the peasant. He wrote in 1798 that the peasant

1   might well have complained [about conscription and requisitioning] but
    he has sold his remaining foodstuffs at extraordinary prices and for
    three years has been able to settle his lease with the modest produc-
    tion of the farmyard . . . As for the more intelligent kind of cultivator
5   knowing how to read and write, he has been called to municipal office.
    This has flattered him and the satisfaction derived from issuing orders
    has given him a taste for the new regime and he has attached himself to
    it.

e) Urban Workers and the Poor

The *sans-culottes* had welcomed the Revolution and had done a great deal to ensure that it was successful. They were to be bitterly disappointed by the first fruits of the Revolution. Many became unemployed as the *parlements* were closed and nobles emigrated. Guilds were abolished in 1791, which was of benefit to apprentices but not their masters. Those still in work were forbidden to strike. In 1793, the Committee of Public Safety gave way to many of their demands, such as a maximum price on bread. However, the bourgeois revolutionary leaders were not prepared in the long run to grant most of what they wanted. The urban workers disliked a free, market economy yet this was imposed on them in 1794, with the result that prices rose dramatically. The bad harvest and harsh winter of 1794–5 reduced them to despair and the risings of Germinal and Prairial, which were crushed. After that workers played no political role in the Revolution. Their economic fortunes continued to decline in 1797, owing to the inflation caused by the fall of the *assignats*. Wages rose but much more slowly than prices. There was, however, a revival in the last years of the Directory from 1797 to 1799, when deflation ensured that real wages were higher than they had been for a very long time. These were also years of good harvests, when the price of bread dropped to two sous a pound (it was 14 sous in July 1789).

The poor suffered more than most during the Revolution. In normal times about a quarter of the population of big cities relied on poor relief. This number increased with the rise in unemployment, yet at the same time their means of obtaining relief were disappearing. The main source of help for the poor had been the Church, which had paid for this out of income from the tithe. When the tithe was abolished and church lands nationalised, the Church could no longer pay for aid to the poor. If the poor were ill they had been cared for in hospitals also provided by the Church and these were affected in the same way by the Church's loss of income. They closed. The Constitution of 1793 said that all citizens had a right to public support but revolutionary governments were always short of money and nothing was done. As late as 1847 the number of hospitals in France was 42 per cent less than in 1789, though the population was seven million more. The result of the decline in the Church's role in providing poor relief and hospitals was that the poor were unable to cope with the economic crisis of 1794–5, when a bad harvest was followed by a harsh winter. Many died, either from starvation or from diseases, which the undernourished could not fight off. In Rouen the mortality rate doubled in 1795–6 and trebled the year after. There was also a marked rise in the number of suicides. The poor responded in the only ways they knew: they joined bands of brigands, which were endemic in many parts of France in the last years of the Directory.

2 The Economy

> **KEY ISSUE** In what way did the French Revolution affect the French economy?

Marxists believe that by getting rid of feudalism, ending the monopolies of the guilds and unifying the national market, the Revolution, in Soboul's words, 'marked a decisive stage in the transition from feudalism to capitalism'. Many historians oppose this interpretation. Alfred Cobban in particular rejects this view. He contends that the revolution was '. . . not for but against capitalism'.[4] They maintain that the Revolution retarded, rather than promoted, the development of capitalism in France and that it was an economic disaster. The most rapidly expanding sector of the French economy up to 1791 was overseas trade. In that year a slave revolt broke out on the West Indian island of San Domingo, which provided three-quarters of France's colonial trade. This was followed in 1793 by war with Britain, when the French coast was blockaded. Prosperous Atlantic seaports such as Bordeaux and Nantes suffered severely, as did the industries in the hinterland – sugar refineries, linen and tobacco manufacture – which had depended on them. In 1797 France had only 200 ocean-going vessels, a tenth of the number of 1789. French exports fell by 50 per cent in the 1790s. Foreign trade had accounted for 25 per cent of France's gross domestic product in 1789: by 1796 it was down to nine per cent.

War had a varied effect on French industries. Some benefited, as there was a demand for cloth for uniforms and iron and coal for the production of arms. The cotton industry gained most of all. It had been virtually ruined by English competition but with the war and French conquests it revived. English goods were kept out of territories under French control, so that French cotton production increased four-fold between the 1780s and 1810. This, however, was a short-term gain and could not be sustained. Once the war was over in 1815 cotton was hit again by British competition and some of the largest French manufacturers went bankrupt. During the war there was a shift in the location of industries from the Atlantic to the Rhine. This favoured cities such as Strasbourg, which grew rich on the continental transit trade. But other areas and industries did not do so well. Supplies of raw materials were disrupted by the war and foreign markets were lost. The linen industry in Brittany (which had exported to the West Indies and South America) fell by a third, industrial production at Marseille decreased by three-quarters. By 1799 production had fallen overall to two-thirds of its pre-war level. A further misfortune suffered by industry was the inflation of 1792–7, which meant that there was little investment. When paper money was withdrawn in 1797 industry faced other problems. There was a shortage of cash, interest rates were high and agricultural prices (and therefore the peasant market for industrial goods) collapsed.

Agriculture stagnated during the Revolution. Production kept pace with population growth but this was done by bringing more land into cultivation rather than by improving productivity, which did not rise until the 1840s. Yields remained low and old-fashioned techniques continued. Oxen were still used for pulling wooden (not metal) ploughs and the harvest was cut with sickles rather than scythes. Most peasants produced for subsistence only and plots remained small, especially when on his death, by law, a peasant's land was divided up equally amongst his sons.

The Revolution held up the development of the French economy, which grew only slowly down to the 1840s. Per capita agricultural production fell during the period with a veritable collapse occurring between 1792 and 1795. It was only by the end of the empire that French agriculture recovered the levels it had reached in 1789. Industrial production was in 1800 not yet back at the level it had reached in 1789.[5] Although France had fallen behind Britain industrially by 1789, the gap between them increased even more markedly during the Revolution. Disruption and dislocation due to the war undoubtedly contributed towards this. The loss of between 1.5 and 2 million people would also have had a profound affect on the economy – reducing the market and the labour force. It was not until the coming of the railways that French industrialists could take advantage of a national market. Railways lowered the cost of transport and gave a great boost to the heavy industries of coal, iron and steel. Only then did factory production become the norm. This happened between 1830 and 1870 and brought to an end the economic *ancien régime*, something the Revolution had failed to do.

3 The Impact on the French Army and Warfare

> **KEY ISSUE** Did the French revolution change the nature of warfare and military organisation?

In a number of ways, the events started in 1789 transformed warfare and military organisation, and its impact would certainly outlast the French Revolution. The challenge to the privileges and power of the *ancien régime* gave social and political prominence to the rights of ordinary citizens. Alongside these newly acquired rights and status, there were obligations. Military service from having been the lot of a small section of society could now in theory be truly universal. Armies might fight with the same weapons but their reserves of available manpower could be dramatically increased and their reasons for waging war 'identified self-interest with the interests of the state'.[6] One of the most important of these was that the citizens of the nation should take a prominent role in its defence, against both its internal and external enemies Not only did the armies of France preserve the republic, they went on to launch a period of almost unparalleled conquest in modern European history, under the leadership of its most talented and ambitious commander – Napoleon Bonaparte. War and conquest were not an end in themselves since the army helped spread the principles of 1789 in its wake, as it attempted to consolidate the Revolution. The French Revolution also witnessed the appearance with the *levée en masse*, of a new concept in European history – that of total war. During the military crisis in the summer of 1793, the whole nation was placed at the service of the state, for the defence of the state.

It is possible to identify three areas where the impact of the Revolution was both obvious and significant in relation to the army and warfare. The first area relates to the expansion and organization of the army. In 1789 the royal army was very unrepresentative of the nation. Over 90 per cent of its officers were noblemen (who comprised between 0.5 to 1.5 per cent of the population). The majority of recruits were drawn from urban areas, only a quarter were peasants (as opposed to 80 per cent of the population). The army was also disproportionately young – over half were under twenty five. As the Revolution progressed, its loyalty to the crown declined, most notably following the Flight to Varennes. Alongside the regular army, there emerged a new force – the National Guard. It came to symbolise the revolution and the growing power of the bourgeoisie. In 1793 these two forces amalgamated – regular soldiers and volunteers. When revolutionary enthusiasm was married to professional military standards an enormously powerful and effective force was created. Against the challenge of external enemies, the call to arms was answered by hundreds of thousands of young Frenchmen. Numbers of volunteers initially, greatly exceeded expectations. By the winter of 1792 France had over 450,000 men in arms, a figure that would rise to over 750,000 by the summer of 1794. Although these figures fluctuated, largely through desertions, the sheer size of these military forces was both impressive and intimidating.

Not only did the army increase in size but secondly, its very nature changed as a result of the Revolution. The army came to embrace the beliefs and values of the Revolution. In defending the republic it was elevated in status and esteem in the eyes of the public. It clearly adopted the principle of careers open to talent. Rapid and well-rewarded promotion for recruits from even the humblest of social backgrounds was an attractive possibility for ambitious career orientated young men. If class was no longer a barrier to promotion, then neither was age. Joubert, Jourdan and Soult were all generals by the age of thirty. Many an ordinary soldier would aspire to hold a field-marshal's baton, if few would ever attain it. Almost a quarter of the generals promoted during the revolution had been Non Commissioned Officers. There was no better role model than Bonaparte himself. The Army of the Republic became very aware of its political role. Successive waves of recruits, particularly the politically active *sans culottes* from Paris and other cities, brought with them a passionate commitment to the cause and principles of 1789, and a willingness to die for *la patrie*. The Representatives on Mission had considerable powers to enforce the political beliefs of the republic. A military force, enthused with revolutionary zeal, allied to a belief in the justice of its cause and bound together in the defence of its nation was unknown in Europe. Within France the success and achievements of the army was genuinely popular with most people.

The third area relates to military tactics, strategy and organization.

New methods were adopted to organize the army during war. French infantry marched into battle in columns, then organized into lines in order to fire, before reforming into columns. The development of the attack column gave commanders much grater mobility, although at the expense of firepower. To try to compensate for this, horse artillery was introduced in 1791–2. French armies developed a new tactic to great effectiveness, – the use of light infantry to support the attack columns. Light infantry was deployed in patrolling and raiding – tactics known as skirmishing. These soldiers needed to be loyal, self-reliant and able to operate with a measure of independence. The high level of commitment and morale within the army particularly among the infantry allowed officers to disperse their soldiers for operational purposes into small groups. These operated very effectively but the tactic was only possible because of good discipline and a high level of motivation among the men.

4 The Territorial and Ideological Impact on Europe

> **KEY ISSUE** What was the territorial and ideological impact of the French Revolution on Europe?

One effect of the French Revolution was that it changed the map of Europe. France temporarily annexed a large amount of territory, although all of this, except Avignon, was lost in 1815. Elsewhere changes were made which were lasting. The city states of Genoa and Venice never recovered an independent existence and Austria's loss of Belgium was permanent. The Holy Roman Empire was abolished and the process of redrawing the map of Germany was begun by getting rid of the ecclesiastical states. Outside Europe, the revolutionary wars had led to Britain seizing Ceylon (Sri Lanka) and the Cape of Good Hope (South Africa), territories she was to retain into the twentieth century.

It can be argued that the most important ideological legacy of the revolution was democratic republicanism. However, the violent and bloody birth of the first republic did alienate many French and a significant number of Europeans. Republicanism became synonymous with Jacobinism and Terror. The French Revolution had a profound affect upon the ideas people held and therefore on the policies they pursued. The veteran radical Dr Richard Price remarked that he was thankful to have lived to see such an eventful and inspirational period. He hoped that British reformers would also take the initiative. But the changes were not all that might have been expected. When so many established institutions, beliefs and practices were attacked – monarchies, religion, privilege – some writers came to their defence and the ideology of conservatism was born. Edmund Burke defended tradition, religious faith and slow change. He argued that violent revolutions produced chaos and ultimately tyranny:

> I do not know under what description to class the present ruling authority in France. It affects to be a pure democracy, though I think it in a direct train of becoming shortly a mischievous and ignoble oligarchy (rule by a minority).[7]

Burke influenced the work of, among others, the Austrian statesman Metternich after 1815. Rulers, who had supported reform in the 1780s, now regarded it as dangerous and so there was a conservative reaction which lasted well into the nineteenth century.

Conservative ideas were not the only ones produced by the French Revolution. Wherever French armies went there was a great diffusion of French ideas and methods, as they created republics, established representative government, seized church lands and abolished privilege. These reforms could be, and often were, reversed when the French withdrew. But ideas could not be eradicated so easily. Concepts such as the sovereignty of the people, equality before the law, freedom from arbitrary arrest, freedom of speech and association and careers open to talent all had a wide appeal. Many of these ideas were ignored in practice during the Revolution but they nevertheless contributed to the revolutionary myth, which influenced so many people outside France, particularly middle-class liberals. Liberalism in the nineteenth century owed much to the French Revolution: 'The Revolution did leave its mark, most visibly in politics and political culture: the practice and ethos of republicanism; the new networks of friendships and associations; the dream of an education that could belong entirely to the city of man. This legacy of the revolutionary struggle certainly marked the long-term.'[8]

Nationalism was another powerful force which the French Revolution produced. Revolutionary leaders had deliberately set out to create a unified nation, by getting rid of all provincial privileges, internal customs duties and different systems of law. Sovereignty, said the Declaration of Rights, resides in the nation. Symbols such as the *tricolore* (the new national flag of France), the *Marseillaise* (adopted as the French national anthem in 1795), huge national festivals, (the first of which was the *Fête de la Fédération* on 14 July 1790 to celebrate the fall of the Bastille), were all used to rouse patriotic fervour. Army life also helped to create loyalty to the nation. Time served in the army was often the first occasion on which peasants had been outside their own locality or had come into contact with the French language (inhabitants of Brittany for example spoke Breton). However, the success of revolutionary leaders in uniting the nation should not be exaggerated. As late as the Third Republic (1871) peasants in the south and west still had local rather than national loyalties and looked on people from outside their area as unwelcome 'foreigners'. Yet France's success in her wars was often attributed to nationalism and the *élan* of the French soldier. Many outside of France were inspired by the right to self-determination which the French proclaimed. In Italy national feeling was aroused for the first time, partly by the French example, and in Germany people also began to look to the formation of a united Germany. A great legacy of the French Revolution was the right to resist oppression, which was enshrined in the Constitution of 1793. Kolokotrones, a Greek bandit and patriot, said that according to his judgement

1 the French Revolution and the doings of Napoleon opened the eyes of the world. The nations knew nothing before and the people thought that kings were gods upon the earth and that they were bound to say that whatever they did was well done. Through this present change it is
5 more difficult to rule the people.

The definitive reply to Edmund Burke's attack on the revolution, was Thomas Paine's *The Rights of Man*, published in 1791. The first half of the nineteenth century became the 'Age of Revolutions' largely because the French provided a model, which others sought to copy. Paine supported the principle of change when he commented:

Every age and generation must be free to act for itself in all cases as the ages and generations which preceded it. The variety and presumptions of governing beyond the grave is the most ridiculous and insolent of all tyrannies.[9]

References

1   Michel Vovelle, *The Revolution Against the Church. From Reason to Supreme Being* (Polity Press, 1991) p. 175.
2   Albert Soboul, *Understanding The French Revolution* (New York, 1989) p. 15.
3   Peter Jones, *The Peasants Revolt?* (History Today Vol 39 May 1989) p. 18.
4   Alfred Cobban, *The Social Interpretation of the French Revolution* (Cambridge, 1964) p. 172.
5   Florin Aftalion, *The French Revolution. An Economic Interpretation* (Cambridge, 1990) p. 191.
6   Hew Strachan, 'The Nation in Arms' quoted in Geoffrey Best (ed), *The Permanent Revolution. The French Revolution and its Legacy 1789–1989* (Fontana, 1988) p. 50.
7   Edmund Burke, *Reflections on the Revolution in France* (1790).
8   Emmet Kennedy, *A Cultural History of the French Revolution* (Yale, 1989) p. 391.
9   Thomas Paine, *The Rights of Man*, 1791 quoted in Robert Gould, *The Impact of Revolution and Revolutionary War on France and Europe* (University of Wales, Aberystwyth, 1993) p. 43.

Summary Diagram
The Impact of the Revolution

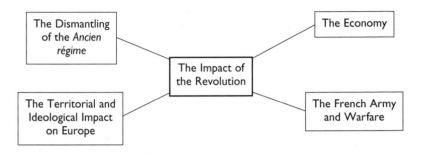

Working on Chapter 7

It is assumed that by the time you read this chapter you will be near-ing the end of your course. You will have studied the French Revolution in some depth and will hopefully have a good under-standing of what actually occurred between c1789 and 1799. Your studies should have covered not only internal events relating to France but the wider international context of how the revolution impacted upon Europe, primarily as a consequence of the revol-utionary war. The chapter draws together the information you will need in order to address the issue of change over time, and in par-ticular what the consequences of an event were. One approach which you might consider to help your understanding of the nature and scale of the changes caused by the revolution is to construct a grid. In one column consider the position during the *ancien régime* while in other columns note what occurred during particular phases of the revolution.

Ancien régime Constitutional Monarchy The First Republic
The Church

Answering essay and structured questions on Chapter 7

The content of this chapter is likely to provide examiners with an opportunity to devise synoptic type questions. In the present exam structure, these questions will be set at the end of your course, on the A2 paper. Synoptic assessment will test your ability to draw together factual knowledge and understanding of concepts (such as cause and consequence, continuity and change) in order to demon-strate overall historical understanding over a period of time. Questions will examine themes and you will be expected to show the connections between different periods, relating to specific issues. Your response will require you to: recall historical knowledge, explain and evaluate interpretations and concepts, assess the significance of individuals, ideas, attitudes etc, and reach a substantiated judgment.

1 To what extent did the French revolution make a significant impact upon Europe in the period 1789–99?

To answer this question you will need to focus carefully on two aspects – firstly, the impact of the internal changes on the monarchy and how these were perceived by other European powers, and, secondly, the impact of the revolutionary war. The key word is 'significant'. Was the impact of relatively short duration or was it irreversible? Note in particular the new ideas which were born.

2 How different was the France of 1799 from that of 1789?

The main theme considered by this question is continuity and change. In preparing for this question draw up a list of the key features of France in 1789 (before the Revolution). You should aim to cover 1) society, 2) the church, 3) government, 4) the legal system and, 5) the economy. Draw up a second list for 1799 and note areas where there were changes. While your work may suggest that there was only change, one area where there certainly was a measure of continuity was control of trade and commerce.

It may be that examiners will use the themes covered by this chapter to devise structured questions of a synoptic nature and spanning the period. The following are two examples of possible questions:

1 a) What was the relationship between the Catholic church and the French state before 1789? (8 marks)
   b) To what extent had the church been affected by revolutionary change between 1789 and 1799? (12 marks)
2 a) Outline the nature of French agriculture and industry during the ancien régime. (8 marks)
   b) How great an impact did the Revolution have upon industry and agriculture during the period 1789–1799? (12 marks)

8 Interpreting the French Revolution

POINTS TO CONSIDER

More than any of the other chapters you have studied, this one is aimed at encouraging further reading and discussion. It is aimed at A level students who have studied the revolution. Few events in modern European history can claim to have had the impact of the French Revolution. The significance of the French Revolution and its interpretation and role in political development is the key theme of this final chapter. Since the early nineteenth century it has been interpreted in a number of different ways. You will be introduced to the Marxist interpretation, and to those who have questioned this way of interpreting history. Since the bicentennial celebrations in 1989 new challenges to existing positions have been made. If you can spare the time, it would be very helpful for you to take the opportunity to read some of the additional references mentioned in the bibliography.

1 The Study of the French Revolution

KEY ISSUE Who were the main writers on the French Revolution up to the First World War?

From its very outset, even before it had fully gathered momentum, contemporaries, mesmerised by the force and power of the Revolution, were either sounding cautionary notes or singing its praises. Edmund Burke wrote a passionate account (*Reflections on the Revolution in France*, 1790) warning the French, that the forces they had unleashed would ultimately end up in dictatorship. The main counter to Burke's view was Thomas Paine's *The Rights of Man* (1791), which became a bestseller (it sold 200,000 copies, which was a huge number for the time). These are among the earliest works relating to the revolution. In the years after the ending of the Revolution the steady trickle of books became a torrent. The historiography of the French Revolution is now a valid source of study in itself. Some of the key elements will be noted in this chapter.

During the nineteenth century as France continued to witness successive political upheavals – in 1830, 1848 and 1870-71, historians sought to interpret the Revolution in terms of the issues which were important at the time. Jules Michlet's seven-volume history of the Revolution was published over the course of the Second Republic and he reflected the views of republican democrats.[1] Proof, if it were needed, of the growing academic status of the study of the revolution, came with the creation of a Chair of the French Revolution at the Sorbonne University in Paris, during the Centennial celebrations in 1889. The first professor appointed to this prestigious chair was Alphonse Aulard. He was the first to apply to the study of the Revolution a rigorous, systematic and critical use of sources.[2] Most of these early historians were writing history from the perspective of the main figures and wielders of power in the Revolution – leading Jacobins, the King's Ministers, the Girondins and so on. This approach is usually termed 'history from above'. The Revolution was seen as a power struggle between rival factions or groups – the *parlements*, the nobility, the middle class. Very little attention was paid to economic issues or to the peasantry and the urban working class.

In the first half of the twentieth century there was a clear shift in emphasis in the way the Revolution was studied. Works were produced on economic and social issues. The roles of the peasantry and the *sans culottes* were carefully examined. Emphasis on ordinary individuals and social groups at the base of society led to the growth of 'history from below'. Some of the impetus for this research came towards the end of the nineteenth century, with the socialist revival and the emergence of Marxism as new political ideologies in search of credible historical roots. In France, the first historian to follow this new direction was Jean Jaures, secretary of the French Socialist Party.[3] The Bolshevik revolution in Russia in 1917 generated further interest in aspects of the French Revolution which were perceived to have been early versions of communism. Russian historians and their French counterparts were particularly interested in Babeuf and Roux and the 'socialist' features of the Jacobin republic.

2 The Marxist Interpretation

> **KEY ISSUE** What is the Marxist interpretation of the French Revolution?

The dominant interpretation of the French Revolution for much of the last hundred years has been the Marxist interpretation. This was most clearly expressed nearly 60 years ago by Georges Lefebvre, and later by his disciple Albert Soboul. Lefebvre regarded the French Revolution as a bourgeois revolution. The commercial and industrial bourgeoisie had been growing in importance in the eighteenth century and had become stronger economically than the nobility. However, their economic strength was not reflected in their position in society. They were kept out of positions of power by the privileged nobility and they resented their inferior position. Therefore, a class struggle developed between the rising bourgeoisie and the declining aristocracy, whose poorer members clung to their privileges with desperate tenacity. The bourgeoisie were able to win this struggle because the monarchy became bankrupt owing to the cost of the wars in which it had fought, especially the American War of Independence.

The French Revolution was above all, according to Lefebvre, a struggle for equal rights. In this conflict the bourgeoisie needed the support of the population of Paris, as the King tried to use force to crush them. He was prevented by a popular rising in Paris, during which the Bastille fell in July 1789. The peasants entered the struggle, largely as a result of the bad harvest of 1788, and this led to the King losing control of the countryside.

These upheavals were followed by widespread reforms between 1789 and 1791, when the institutions of the old regime were abolished and replaced by a new administrative structure, much of which still remains. However, the Revolution did not come to an end, because the King and the aristocracy did not accept what had happened. A turning point came when war was declared on Austria in 1792. The King and Queen were accused of intriguing with the enemy and this led to the fall of the monarchy and the execution of the King. The war also led to a three-fold crisis, from which it appeared that the Revolution would not survive. An economic crisis resulted from the printing of more and more paper money to pay for the war. This led to inflation and popular discontent. Conscription was decreed in order to provide soldiers: resistance to it caused civil war in the Vendée. The third crisis occurred when the war went badly and foreign armies invaded France. Lefebvre saw the Terror as a response to these crises. Desperate measures were needed and these included executing the enemies of the Republic.

The support of the *sans-culottes* was needed for a successful war effort, so many of their demands were granted. However, the interests of the bourgeois leaders of the Revolution and the *sans-culottes* were different. The former believed in laissez-faire – a market free from government interference – whereas the latter wanted control of prices. A clash was, therefore, inevitable, particularly as the bourgeoisie had no intention of allowing the *sans-culottes* to take control of the Revolution. Robespierre began to cut back the power of the *sans-culottes* and executed some of their leaders but it was after his fall that the class interests of the bourgeoisie were shown most clearly. All controls on prices were removed. As a result, there was massive inflation and, in Germinal and Prairial 1795, the starving *sans-culottes* rose in despair. These risings were crushed and this marked the end of the *sans-culottes* as a political force during the Revolution.

The threat to the new government, the Directory, came from the monarchists. They staged a rising in Vendémiaire 1795, which was crushed by the army. The army was called in again in 1797 to purge the elected Councils, after electoral gains by the monarchists. As the

Directory began to lose control of the country and brigandage spread, the bourgeoisie turned to a strong man in the army to secure their gains from the Revolution. In the *coup d'état* of Brumaire in 1799 Napoleon brought the Revolution to an end.

The Marxist interpretation of the revolution as a class struggle gained added strength from the study of history from below. Georges Lefebvre was the real initiator of research into the role of ordinary people during the revolutionary period. His focus was the French countryside. Lefebvre in 1924 was the first to show that the peasants were not a monolithic bloc but consisted of different groups whose interests were often opposed to one another. Landless peasants and sharecroppers, for example, were usually hostile to the large tenant farmers, whom they called the 'rural bourgeoisie'. The Revolution increased, rather than reduced, these differences.

A seminal work published in 1958 was Albert Soboul's study of the Parisian *sans culottes* in Year II. He set a whole new standard for research into ordinary working people in urban areas during the Revolution.[4] Soboul's work challenged the view that ordinary people were an undifferentiated mass, who reacted predictably (by rioting) to food shortages and who followed the political lead of the upper classes. They were not seen as having any ideas or institutions of their own. Soboul did for urban dwellers, in *The Parisian Sans-culottes of the Year II* (1958), what Lefebvre had done for the peasants. He was soon followed by George Rudé's *The Crowd in the French Revolution* (1959) and Richard Cobb's *The People's Armies* (in two volumes 1961 and 1963). These historians looked at the popular movement and rejected the common description of it as 'a mob'. They saw that it had its own institutions and its own ideas and attitudes, which were very different from those of the bourgeois leaders of the Revolution. Soboul studied the clubs and revolutionary committees and showed how the *sans-culottes* made the Revolution more radical and why they were destroyed by the Terror they had done so much to create. His study of the revolutionary period, *The French Revolution 1787–1799* (1962) has been described as the 'high watermark of the socialist interpretation of the French revolution'.[5] According to the American historian Robert Darnton, his analysis 'still stands as the best explanation of the climactic phase of the Revolution'. Rudé studied the social groups which formed the 'crowd', whilst Cobb (who is not a Marxist) discussed the revolutionary armies of the popular movement. All these historians showed that the *sans-culottes* were a vital revolutionary force, particularly in the years 1792–4.

3 Revisionist Interpretations

> **KEY ISSUE** How have the revisionist historians challenged the
> Marxist interpretation?

The Marxist account of the Revolution was generally accepted until the
1960s. It was challenged by a group of 'revisionist' (anti-Marxist) historians. The first important critic was the English historian Alfred Cobban
in his, *The Social Interpretation of the French Revolution* (1964). Cobban
questioned the validity of the social interpretation, and also whether the
revolution was led by a rising bourgeoisie. He pointed out that the revolutionary bourgeoisie were not businessmen or merchants (i.e. capi-
talists) but were lawyers and other professional men, many of whom
were office-holders. He showed that the capitalist bourgeoisie were not
leaders of the Revolution and that they gained little from it. Far from
leading to the triumph and extension of capitalism, the Revolution
retarded the development of capitalism in France for a generation. In
1799 industry remained small-scale and most peasants aimed simply at
subsistence farming, as they had done before the Revolution.

Support for Cobban's views came from the American historian
George Taylor who denied that there was a class conflict between the
nobility and bourgeoisie. He maintained that both groups before the
Revolution shared the same values and invested in the same things,
such as land and government offices, which could be bought.[6] As all
rich bourgeois could buy offices, many of which conferred nobility,
what they wanted to do was join the nobility rather than to get rid of
it. Both nobles and rich bourgeois formed part of the same élite. The
idea that the fortunes of nobles in the eighteenth century were declining compared with those of the bourgeoisie, has also been attacked.
There were some poor nobles but the richest people in France, at the
end of the eighteenth century as at the beginning, were nobles.

The best known of the Revisionist historians was François Furet.
His book *Interpreting the French Revolution* (1981) inspired more than
almost any other, research into the French Revolution during the
1980s and 1990s. Furet was much influenced by Alexis de
Tocqueville's *The Ancien Régime and the French Revolution* (1856). He
went beyond merely questioning the economic and social interpretations of the revolution as a class-based struggle, favoured by the
Marxists, to considering the intellectual and cultural background to
1789. According to Furet, the driving force for change were the
advanced democratic ideas of Enlightenment philosophers, such as
Rousseau. He argued that the Revolution adopted a radical ideology
of popular sovereignty so that any misuse of power could be justified,
as long as it was carried out in the name of the people. The collective
will of the state was used to explain away all manner of abuses, particularly those undertaken during the Terror. Furet during the bicen-

tennial celebrations urged that the time was now ripe to end politically inspired interpretations of the revolution. As he declared 'The Revolution is over'. 'In the political arena of present day France, nothing nor anyone is threatening the achievements of the French revolution . . . no historical debate about the revolution any longer involves any real political stakes'.[7]

The counter-revolution (the opposition to the Revolution), which sometimes took the form of open revolt, has also been considered by some revisionist historians. In doing so they have changed the way we look at the Revolution. They have shown that the counter-revolution had little to do with British agents or aristocratic plots. It was a widespread, lasting and popular movement, which covered large areas of France from 1793 to 1797 and helps to explain much of what happened during those years: repression, the Terror, the failure of constitutional government between 1794 and 1797, and the need for a dictator in 1799.

4 Trends and Developments

> **KEY ISSUE** What are recent trends in the debate on the French Revolution?

Some of the revisionist attacks on the Marxist interpretation were not, to begin with based on detailed archival research. Less emphasis appeared to be placed on serious scholarship and more on a 'general assault of the Marxist paradigm (model) of the Revolution'.[8] Gwynne Lewis's criticism of the contribution of the revisionists concerns 'the way in which they have ignored or down-graded the importance of the social question during the 1790s.'[9] He believes that it was the involvement of the peasants, artisans and shopkeepers which provided the main dynamic of the Revolution in its early years.

What, then, remains of the Marxist interpretation of the Revolution? A great deal, including the four-fold revolution of 1787–9, the account of the fall of the monarchy and the role played by the *sans-culottes* during the Revolution. Much of the revisionist criticism has been concerned with the origins of the Revolution and with its results. Here much of the Marxist interpretation has been abandoned. The idea that the Revolution was a class war of bourgeoisie versus aristocrats has had to be discarded, as has the idea that the Revolution led to the dominance of the capitalist bourgeoisie and the development of capitalism. Yet the Revolution was a bourgeois revolution, in that all the revolutionary leaders (certainly after 1791) were bourgeois and the bourgeoisie were the chief beneficiaries of the Revolution. They were the ones who bought most of the church lands which were sold, and who benefited from the increase in career opportunities open to talent, which enabled them to occupy all the high offices of state. They were not the only ones to benefit. All peasants who were landowners benefited by the abolition of feudal dues – about 4 million families or 18 million people out of a population of 28 million. So the Revolution was not the 'disaster' depicted by some revisionist historians.

What are the recent trends in research on the French Revolution? Two are worth noting. Firstly, since 1989 the work of the revisionist historians has been challenged by the Neo-Liberals. They differ from the revisionists in that they do not minimise the oppressive character of the eighteenth-century nobility. Also they argue that the violence and upheval of the early years of the revolution was necessary 'to the establishment of a liberal and free state'.[10] Secondly, there has been much research into the role of women during the revolutionary period – an area which has been overlooked for far too long.

Whether or not a post-revisionist consensus on the causes and events of the French Revolution is ever possible, let alone desirable, is debatable. What this short chapter has tried to do is to acquaint you with some of the historiographical trends in the study of the French Revolution. It is easy to feel intimidated by the monumental scale of the work that has already been undertaken. Do not be daunted by this. In the last analysis you should try to enjoy the period for what it was, which according to the politician, Charles James Fox was 'the greatest event that has happened in the history of the world'. (30 July 1789)

References

1 Jules Michelet, *Histoire de la Révolution française*, 7 volumes, 1847–53.
2 George Rudé, *Interpretations of the French Revolution* (Historical Association no. 47, 1961) p. 11.
3 Jean Jaures, *Histoire socialiste de la Révolution française, 1901–4.*
4 Albert Soboul, *The Parisian Sans-culottes and the French Revolution 1793–4* (Oxford, 1964).
5 Gwynne Lewis, Introduction to Albert Soboul *The French Revolution 1787–1799* (Unwin Hyman,1989) p. xii.
6 George V. Taylor, *Types of Capitalism in Eighteenth Century France* (English Historical Review 79, 1964) pp. 478–97.
7 Francois Furet, *Interpreting the French Revolution* (Cambridge University Press, 1981) p. 82.
8 Geoffrey Ellis, *The 'Marxist Interpretation' of the French Revolution* (English Historical Review, April 1978) p. 363.
9 Gwynne Lewis, *The French Revolution Rethinking the Debate* (Routledge, 1993) p. 112.
10 Gary Kates (ed), *Introduction to The French Revolution Recent Debates and New Controversies* (Routledge, 1998) p. 12.

Summary Diagram
Interpreting the French Revolution

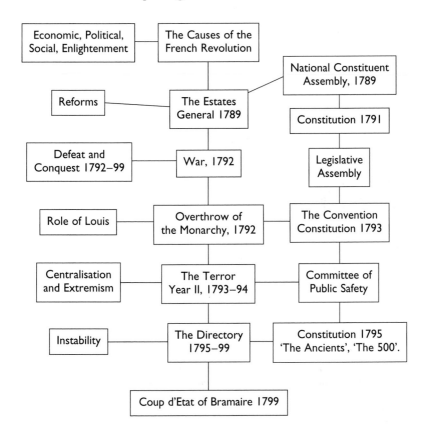

Economic, Political, Social, Enlightenment

The Causes of the French Revolution

National Constituent Assembly, 1789

Reforms

The Estates General 1789

Constitution 1791

Defeat and Conquest 1792–99

War, 1792

Legislative Assembly

Role of Louis

Overthrow of the Monarchy, 1792

The Convention Constitution 1793

Centralisation and Extremism

The Terror Year II, 1793–94

Committee of Public Safety

Instability

The Directory 1795–99

Constitution 1795 'The Ancients', 'The 500'.

Coup d'Etat of Bramaire 1799

Working on Chapter 8

The study of the historiography of any event can be difficult. With a subject as complicated as the French Revolution, the difficulties are compounded. To try to make sense of the various developments which have taken place since the 1790s you may well find it useful, in the first place, simply to tackle the key developments, namely the Marxist and Revisionist interpretations. One approach to dealing with this is to consider a number of questions for each interpretation: **i)** What did each view argue? **ii)** How has each view been challenged? **iii)** Who are the key historians linked to each interpretation? Once you have addressed these questions to your satisfaction, you could then consider new trends and developments in more recent years.

Glossary

aides – duties on food and drink.

armées revolutionnaires – civilian armies in 1793–4, formed to requisition grain from the countryside to feed the cities.

assignat – paper money in general used from 1791–7.

biens nationaux – property of the Church and *émigrés* seized by the state and sold at auction.

cahiers – lists of grievances drawn up by the three Estates in 1788.

capitation – poll tax, paid by all except the clergy.

champart – harvest dues paid by peasants to their *seigneurs*.

Chouans – peasants who fought against the Revolution.

cockade – rosette in red, white and blue, revolutionary symbol.

Commune – the municipal government of Paris.

corvée – the peasants' obligation to do unpaid labour on the roads.

coup d'état – an attempt to seize power and overthrow the state.

don gratuit – 'free gift' from the Church instead of paying taxes.

émigrés – people who had fled from France during the Revolution.

fédérés – National Guardsmen from the provinces.

gabelle – a tax on salt.

généralités – financial areas of the *ancien régime*.

jeunesse dorée – 'gilded youth'. Middle-class youth who took part in the White Terror and attacked Jacobins and *sans-culottes*.

journée – days of action by the *sans-culottes*.

laboureur – a well-off peasant, who grew enough food for his own needs.

lettres de cachet – sealed letters, issued by the King, by which people could be imprisoned without trial.

levée en masse – mobilisation of the whole French nation for war.

lit de justice – ceremony at which the King insisted on the *parlements* registering royal edicts.

livre – main unit of money, the equivalent of 20 *sous*.

lods et ventes – feudal due paid to the *seigneur* when property was sold.

mainmorte – restriction on serfs regarding disposal of property.

maximum – price fixed for grain and basic necessities.

menu peuple – the common people.

Montagnards – Jacobin deputies as they sat on the top seats (The Mountain) in the Assembly.

Muscadin – gilded youth, young royalists.

noblesse de robe – magistrates who had bought enobling offices.

noyades – mass drowning of refractory priests and others in the Loire.

octrois – duties on goods entering towns.

parlements – 13 high courts of appeal which had the right to register royal edicts and criticise them.

pays d'états – provinces near French frontiers which had special rights.

rentier – a person living on *rentes*.

sans-culottes – urban workers: wage-earners and small property owners.

Sections – the 48 units of local self-government in Paris.

taille – the main direct tax for commoners before the Revolution.

vingtième – tax on income, supposedly of five per cent but often more.

Further Reading

Textbooks

There are four outstanding books which cover the French Revolution as a whole:

William Doyle, *The Oxford History of the French Revolution* (OUP 1989);
Francois Furet, *The French Revolution 1770–1814* (Blackwell, 1988) – the leading revisionist historian;
D.M.G. Sutherland, *France 1789–1815: Revolution and Counter-revolution* (Fontana 1985);
As the sub-title implies, this second book treats the opposition to the Revolution much more fully than is usual in general histories of the Revolution;
Albert Soboul, *The French Revolution 1787–1799. From the storming of the Bastille to Napoleon* (Unwin/Hyman,1989) – a classic account from the doyen of the Marxist historians.

Specialist Studies

If you want more detailed understanding of the key phases and aspects of the revolution, then the following is a small selection of the vast academic literature which is available.

a) The *Ancien Régime* and Constitutional Monarchy

P.R. Campbell, *The Ancien Régime in France* (Basil Blackwell, 1988);
W. Doyle, *The Origins of the French Revolution* (OUP, revised edition 1989);
J. Hardman, *French Politics 1774–1779* (London, 1995); **G. Lefebvre**, *The Coming of the French Revolution* (Princeton, 1947); **N. Temple**, *The Road to 1789: From Reform to Revolution in France* (University of Wales Press, 1992) – contains a selection of illustrative documents.

b) The Terror

H. Gough, *The Terror in the French Revolution* (Macmillan,1998); **N. Hampson**, *The Terror in the French Revolution* (Historical Association, 1981); **G.A. Williams**, *Artisans and Sans-Culottes* (Libres, reprinted 1989).

c) The Directory and emergence of Napoleon

M. Crook, *Napoleon Comes to Power* (Univerity of Wales Press, 1998) – plus illustrative documents; **M. Lyons**, *France Under the Directory* (CUP, 1975).

d) Social and Economic aspects

F. Aftalion, *The French Revolution. An Economic Interpretation* (CUP,1990);
A. Cobban, *The Social Interpretation of the French Revolution* (CUP, 1964);

N. **Hampson**, *A Social History of the French Revolution* (Routledge 1966); **P.M. Jones**, *The Peasantry in the French Revolution* (CUP, 1988).

e) Religion and Culture

N. **Aston**, *Religion and Revolution in France 1780–1804* (Macmillan, 2000); **E. Kennedy**, *A Cultural History of the French Revolution* (Yale, 1989); **J. McManners**, *The French Revolution and the Church* (SPCK, 1969).

f) War and the Army

T.C.W., Blanning, *The Origins of the French Revolutionary Wars* (Longman 1986); **R. Cobb**, *The People's Armies* (Yale, 1987).

Biographies

There are very few up to date biographies of the key figures. Among the most recent are: **N. Hampson**, *The Life and Opinions of Maximilien Robespierre* (Duckworth 1974); **J. Hardman** *Louis XVI* (Arnold, 2000); **J.** **Hardman**, *Robespierre* (Longman, 1999).

Historiographical Works

F. **Furet**, *Interpreting the French Revolution* (CUP, 1981); **G. Kates** (ed), *The French Revolution Recent Debates and New Controversies* (Routledge, 1998); **G. Lewis**, *The French Revolution Rethinking the Debate* (Routledge, 1993).

Source collections and reference works

J. **Brooman**, *The Reign of Terror in France. J-B Carrier and the Drownings at Nantes* (Longman, 1986); **L.W. Cowie**, *The French Revolution* (Macmillan Education, 1987); **J. Hardman**, *The French Revolution, 1785–1795* (Arnold, 1981); **D.G. Wright**, *Revolution and Terror in France, 1789–1795* (Longman 1974); **R. Cobb and C. Jones**, *The French Revolution, 1789–1795* (Simon and Schuster, 1989) – This book also contains short and valuable articles on various aspects of the Revolution and some splendid illustrations.
C. **Jones**, *The Longman Companion to the French Revolution* (Longman, 1990) quite simply the best single volume reference work covering the period, an invaluable guide.
S. **Schama**, *Citizens A Chronicle of the French Revolution* (Viking, 1989) no bibliography could be complete without mentioning this massive work in the grand narrative style of history, richly endowed with written and visual sources – dip into it at your leisure and pleasure.

Index